PB96-916202
NTSB/HAR-96/02

NATIONAL TRANSPORTATION SAFETY BOARD

WASHINGTON, D.C. 20594

HIGHWAY/RAILROAD ACCIDENT REPORT

Collision of Northeast Illinois Regional Commuter
Railroad Corporation (METRA) Train and
Transportation Joint Agreement School District 47/155
School Bus at Railroad/Highway Grade Crossing
in Fox River Grove, Illinois, on October 25, 1995

6626C

Abstract: This report explains the collision of a Northeast Illinois Regional Commuter Railroad Corporation commuter train with a Transportation Joint Agreement School District 47/155 school bus that was stopped at a railroad/highway grade crossing in Fox River Grove, Illinois on October 25, 1995. Seven school bus passengers were killed and the bus driver and 24 bus passengers were injured.

From its investigation of this accident, the Safety Board identified the following safety issues: the appropriateness of the busdriver's performance; the adequacy of the school district bus routing and busdriver monitoring and evaluating procedures; the road design; the railroad/highway signal interaction; the coordination and communication between the Illinois Department of Transportation and the Union Pacific Railroad Company and their oversight of the signal system integration; and the injury and survival factors in the school bus.

As a result of its investigation of this accident, the Safety Board made recommendations to the Secretary of Transportation, the Federal Highway Administration, the Federal Railroad Administration, the National Highway Traffic Safety Administration, the State of Illinois, the Illinois Department of Transportation, the Transportation Joint Agreement School District 47/155, the National Association of State Directors of Pupil Transportation Services, the American Association of State Highway and Transportation Officials, the National Association of County Engineers, the American Public Works Association, the Institute of Transportation Engineers, the Association of American Railroads, the American Short Line Railroad Association, the American Public Transit Association, and Operation Lifesaver, Inc. The Safety Board also issued urgent action recommendations following this accident to the Federal Highway Administration, the Federal Railroad Administration, and the State Directors of Transportation.

The National Transportation Safety Board is an independent Federal agency dedicated to promoting aviation, railroad, highway, marine, pipeline, and hazardous materials safety. Established in 1967, the agency is mandated by Congress through the Independent Safety Board Act of 1974 to investigate transportation accidents, determine the probable cause of accidents, issue safety recommendations, study transportation safety issues, and evaluate the safety effectiveness of government agencies involved in transportation. The Safety Board makes public its actions and decisions through accident reports, safety studies, special investigation reports, safety recommendations, and statistical reviews.

PB96-916202

NATIONAL TRANSPORTATION SAFETY BOARD

Washington, D.C. 20594

HIGHWAY/RAILROAD ACCIDENT REPORT

Collision of Northeast Illinois Regional Commuter Railroad Corporation (METRA) Train and Transportation Joint Agreement School District 47/155 School Bus at Railroad/Highway Grade Crossing in Fox River Grove, Illinois, on October 25, 1995

Adopted: October 29, 1996

Notation 6626C

ERRATA

THESE CORRECTIONS SHOULD BE MADE
TO THE PREVIOUSLY PUBLISHED REPORT
IDENTIFIED AS FOLLOWS

HIGHWAY/RAILROAD ACCIDENT REPORT

COLLISION OF NORTHEAST ILLINOIS REGIONAL COMMUTER RAILROAD
CORPORATION (METRA) TRAIN AND TRANSPORTATION JOINT AGREEMENT
SCHOOL DISTRICT 47/155 SCHOOL BUS AT RAILROAD/HIGHWAY GRADE
CROSSING IN FOX RIVER GROVE, ILLINOIS, ON OCTOBER 25,1995

NTSB/HAR-96/02 (PB96-916202)

Page 7, Figure 3: revise injury citation for Bus Body seat immediately behind driver's seat (row 1, seat A), from F-14: AIS-I to

F-14 : AIS-O

Page 61: following text add

BY THE NATIONAL TRANSPORTATION SAFETY BOARD

JAMES E. HALL
Chairman

ROBERT T. FRANCIS II
Vice Chairman

JOHN A. HAMMERSCHMIDT
Member

JOHN J. GOGLIA
Member

GEORGE W. BLACK, JR.
Member

October 29, 1996

CONTENTS

EXECUTIVE SUMMARY

On October 25, 1995, at 7:10 a.m., the Northeast Illinois Regional Commuter Railroad Corporation (d/b/a Metropolitan Rail) express commuter train 624 struck the rear left side of a stopped Transportation Joint Agreement School District 47/155 school bus at a railroad/highway grade crossing in Fox River Grove, Illinois. The accident occurred after the school bus had crossed the railroad tracks and stopped for a red traffic signal, with its rear extended about 3 feet into the path of the train. Of the 35 school bus passengers, 7, 24, and 4 passengers sustained fatal, serious to minor, and no injuries, respectively; the busdriver received minor injuries. The 120 passengers and 3 crewmembers aboard the commuter train were uninjured.

The National Transportation Safety Board determines that the probable cause of the collision was that the busdriver had positioned the school bus so it encroached upon the railroad tracks because of the failure of: 1) the Illinois Department of Transportation to recognize the short queuing area on northbound Algonquin Road and to take corrective action; 2) the Illinois Department of Transportation to recognize the insufficient time of the green signal indication for vehicles on northbound Algonquin Road before the arrival of a train at the crossing; and 3) the Transportation Joint Agreement School District 47/155 to identify route hazards and to provide its drivers with alternative instructions for such situations. Contributing to the accident was the failure of the Illinois Department of Transportation and its many contractors, the Illinois Commerce Commission, and the railroads to have a communication system that ensures understanding of the integration and working relationship of the railroad and highway signal systems.

The major safety issues discussed in this report are: the appropriateness of the busdriver's performance; the adequacy of the school district bus routing and busdriver monitoring and evaluating procedures; the road design; the railroad/highway signal interaction; the coordination and communication between the Illinois Department of Transportation and the Union Pacific Railroad Company and their oversight of the signal system integration; and the injury and survival factors in the school bus.

As a result of its investigation of this accident, the Safety Board makes recommendations to the U.S. Secretary of Transportation, the Federal Highway Administration, the Federal Railroad Administration, the National Highway Traffic Safety Administration, the State of Illinois, the Transportation Joint Agreement School District 47/155, the National Association of State Directors of Pupil Transportation Services, the Illinois Department of Transportation, the American Association of State Highway and Transportation Officials, the National Association of County Engineers, the American Public Works Association, the Institute of Transportation Engineers, the Association of American Railroads, the American Short Line Railroad Association, the American Public Transit Association, and Operation Lifesaver, Inc. The Safety Board also issued urgent action recommendations following this accident to the Federal Highway Administration, the Federal Railroad Administration, and the State Directors of Transportation.

Accident Narrative

About 7:10 a.m. on October 25, 1995, an eastbound Northeast Illinois Regional Commuter Railroad Corporation d/b/a Metropolitan Rail (METRA) express commuter train 624 en route to Chicago, Illinois, collided with the left rear side of a Transportation Joint Agreement (TJA) School District 47/155 school bus at a railroad/highway grade crossing in Fox River Grove, Illinois. (See figure 1.) The collision occurred on Algonquin Road near its intersection with U.S. Route 14 (US 14). The school busdriver had driven across the railroad tracks and stopped for the red indication of a highway traffic signal. The northbound school bus, which was waiting within the available storage space (queuing area), had its left rear extending about 3 feet into the path of the train.

At the time, the Fox River Grove police chief and the Area Traffic Signal Engineer from the Illinois Department of Transportation (IDOT) were in a parked car that faced Algonquin Road to observe the traffic signal at this intersection for train and vehicular traffic problems. The police chief said that: the school bus stopped on the south side of the tracks, proceeded across the tracks, and stopped near the white-painted stop line; it was the only vehicle in the queuing area; the railroad crossing gate came down and bounced against the left side (just to the rear of the center) of the school bus; as the eastbound METRA train approached the crossing, its horn was blowing; and the train struck the rear of the school bus.

Two drivers waiting on the south side of the railroad tracks saw the school bus in the left lane across the tracks. They stated that the traffic light was red when the crossing lights began flashing and the gates came down. They saw the north gate come down and hit the school bus.

Of the 35 school bus passengers, 7 sustained fatal injuries, 24 sustained serious to minor injuries, and 4 were not injured. The school busdriver sustained minor injuries. The estimated 120 passengers and the 3 crewmembers aboard the train were uninjured.

School Bus. — On the day of the accident, the TJA school bus dispatcher called the busdriver to substitute for the regular busdriver, who was ill.[1] Arriving about 6:30 a.m. at the bus garage, the substitute driver was provided a route map on which the street names and the stops were printed. She performed a pretrip inspection of the bus and departed about 6:35 a.m., which was 20 minutes later than the regular departure time.

She had never driven this route before, either in a car or a school bus, when checking routes in her role as the assistant director of transportation.

She made her first stop to pick up passengers at 6:55 a.m. Because she was not familiar with the stops on the route and the map was difficult to read in the predawn darkness, she asked one of these initial passengers to assist her with the route, and he agreed to do so. She had completed all but one stop on the route as the bus approached the grade crossing at Algonquin Road, where she stopped it on the south side of the crossing, activated the hazard lights, opened the bus door, and looked right and left. She said that she did not see a train and therefore closed the door and proceeded over the railroad tracks. The passenger assisting the busdriver was seated directly behind her and said that he looked both ways and saw no train.

---

[1] The regular school busdriver was absent that day, and the regular substitute busdriver had been assigned to another route.

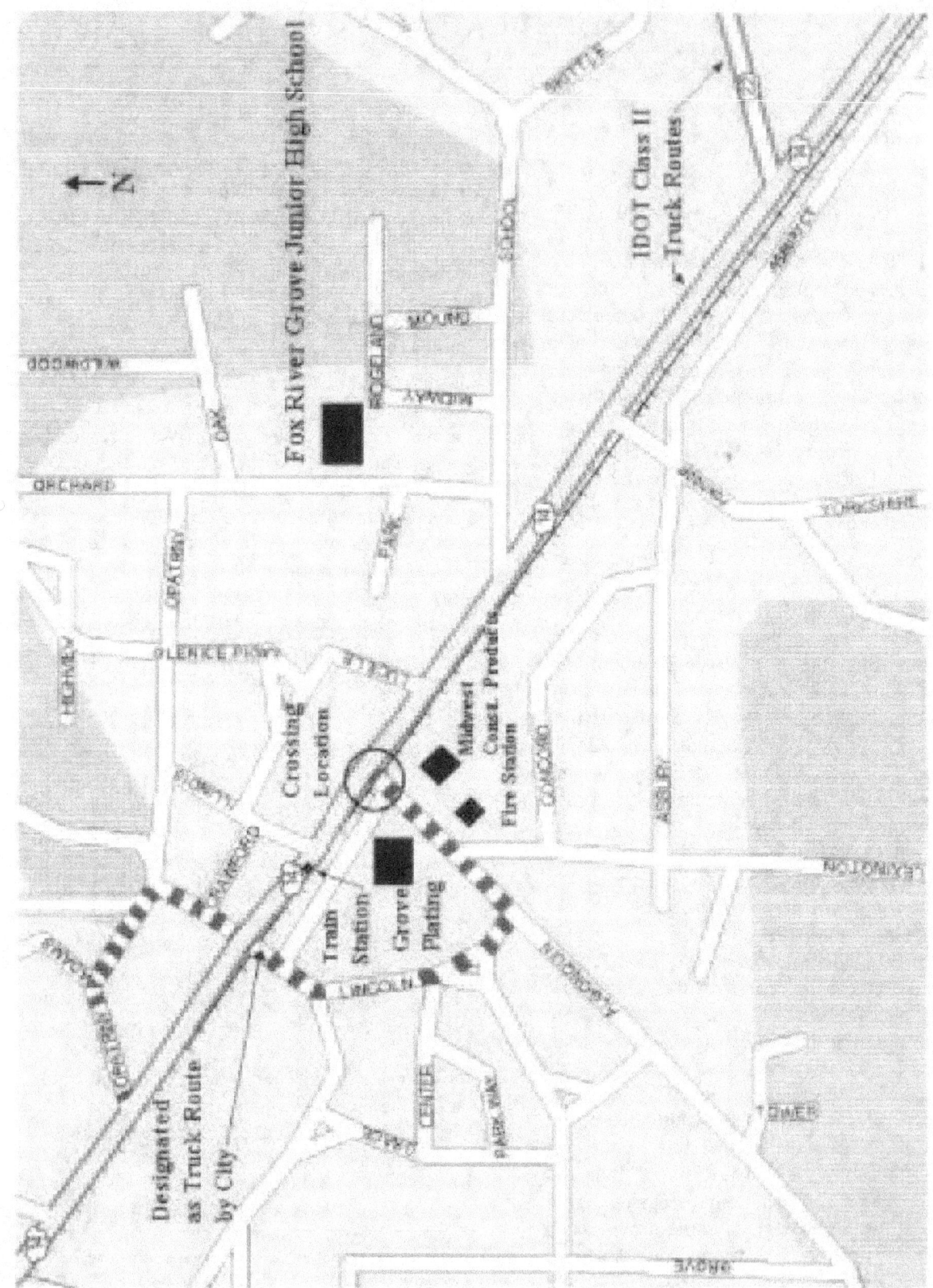

Figure 1 — Map of accident showing route of bus (dotted line).

A traffic signal system controls the intersection at Algonquin Road and US 14. Two railroad tracks cross Algonquin Road about 45 feet south of US 14. The railroad/highway grade crossing is equipped with active crossing warning devices (gates, lights, and bell). Loop detectors,[2] designed to detect the presence of vehicles, are embedded in the pavement on the north and south sides of the tracks.

The busdriver recounted:

I proceeded across the tracks because the light [for Algonquin Road at US 14] was red and I knew I had to go up there [north of the tracks] and trip the sensor in order for the light to turn green to proceed through the intersection. It was like moments that it [the accident] happened.

She said that after the school bus had crossed over the tracks, she did not believe that it was extending into the path of the train and that it appeared to have "plenty of room." In later statements, the busdriver said, "It never entered my mind that there wasn't enough room for that bus to fit."

Most passengers said they had been talking to each other or sleeping during the ride. Some commented that the noise level on the bus "was not any louder than normal" and "was really quiet" and that "people were talking calmly, like in a restaurant, but not real busy." Eight passengers reported that the music broadcast from the AM/FM radio did not interfere with their conversations; nine passengers reported that they heard the train horn. Four said that they saw the crossing warning devices activate, and eight recalled seeing the train before impact. Another four passengers remembered standing up to move forward in the bus just before impact.

From the back of the bus, passengers were yelling, "a train is coming," "we're still on the tracks," "move the bus," and "I think we're gonna get hit by a train," recalled others.

Passengers recalled that such comments were initially made in a joking fashion, but as the train approached the bus, the yelled remarks became serious warnings. The busdriver reported that her passengers were making noise; however, she did not understand that they were warning her that a train was coming and added that she did not hear the train horn, the crossing bell, or the sound of the gate striking the bus. She said that she was not aware that a train was coming until it had struck the bus. The passenger assisting the busdriver with the route recalled, although the busdriver could not, that both the two-way radio with the TJA dispatcher and the AM/FM radio were transmitting. He said that he heard the train horn just before the train struck the bus, and then both he and the busdriver looked up into the rearview mirror at the same time. They then simultaneously exclaimed, "Oh!". He also reported that he observed the crossing gate in the mirror after hearing the train's horn. He said that "... right before the train hit," he became aware of the others on the bus yelling about the train coming.

Several motorists traveling on US 14 reported that their traffic signal at Algonquin Road turned from green to yellow to red just before the collision. However, the busdriver and passengers said that they never saw their traffic signal on Algonquin turn green. Others who witnessed the accident and who could observe the same signal as the busdriver could only state that it was red before the accident and green afterwards.

Train.—The engineer of train 624 reported that after arriving at the METRA terminal in Crystal Lake, Illinois, about 6:30 a.m., he inspected train 624 and its engine and performed an initial terminal air brake test. He was satisfied with the inspection and test, and train 624 departed Crystal Lake on schedule at 7 a.m.

---

[2] *Traffic Engineering Handbook*, Fourth Edition, Institute of Transportation Engineers, 1992. A loop detector has two major components, an amplifier and an in-pavement loop or sensor. The detector amplifier transmits its own energy or electrical field and operates on the principle that a vehicle resting in, or passing over the loop will unbalance a tuned circuit and send an impulse to the amplifier.

The train traveled eastbound at no more than 40 mph as it approached Cary, Illinois, the first station southeast of Crystal Lake. The Cary Station was not a scheduled stop for the train. However, the engineer slowed the speed of train 624 to between 15 and 18 mph, as required by a railroad timetable special instruction, to allow a westbound train from Chicago, which was in the station at the time, to discharge its passengers and to provide time for the departing passengers to cross the tracks. He then had a clear wayside railroad signal (green aspect) just beyond the Cary Station that permitted him to operate the train at a maximum speed of 70 mph.

The engineer said that train 624 was traveling about 66 mph as it crossed the Fox River bridge (about 2,300 feet west of the Algonquin Road grade crossing) when he saw that the school bus had crossed the first track at "a very slow speed." He reported that the sun was coming up over a hill on his left but it did not interfere with his view of the school bus. The engineer considered that if the school bus continued moving at that slow speed, it would clear his train. However, because the school bus was going so slowly, he placed the train throttle in the idle position, made a full-service brake application,[3] and sounded the horn. The engineer stated that when he realized that the school bus had not cleared the second track, he placed his train brakes in emergency application.[4] He said that the bus came to a stop with its rear on the railroad tracks in the path of the train. (See Tests and Research section for more information.)

Collision. —Train 624 struck the school bus in its left rear side, and it rotated counter-clockwise. The bus body and its chassis separated and came to rest with the chassis facing in a northwest direction and the body facing south (approximately 42 feet apart from each other). Gouge marks led up to the final rest position of the bus body. The bus body struck

and knocked down the breakaway traffic light stanchion at the southeast corner of the US 14 intersection. (See figure 2.) Train 624 did not derail, and its cab control car (the lead car) stopped about 1,422 feet east of the point of collision.

Emergency Response

The Fox River Grove police chief, after witnessing the collision, immediately radioed for assistance via his portable radio. After train 624 stopped, its engineer radioed his train dispatcher and reported striking the bus.

The Cary Police Department dispatcher received multiple 911 calls at 7:13 a.m., whereupon he notified the Fox River Grove Fire Department and the Crystal Lake Regional Command Center. Located on Algonquin Road, about 350 feet southeast of the accident site, the Fox River Grove Fire Department responded at 7:18 a.m. with an ambulance, a fire engine, four emergency medical technicians, and two paramedics. The Fox River Grove assistant fire chief arrived on the scene almost immediately and acted as incident commander (IC), requesting the Mutual Aid Box Alarm System[5] third alarm response, which he later upgraded to a fifth alarm response.[6] The IC established a command post in the Algonquin Road and US 14 intersection and triage areas on both sides of the school bus. Shortly after the Fox River Grove Fire Department had arrived on the scene, 20 ambulances from 18 fire departments, as well as 2 helicopters, arrived and transported 32 of the injured passengers to medical facilities. The local hospital activated its disaster plan and dispatched a doctor to the scene at 7:27 a.m.

---

[3] Operation of automatic brake valve in which reducing air pressure in the brake cylinder applies the brake.

[4] Substantial rapid reduction of brake cylinder air pressure initiated to stop train in minimum distance.

---

[5] Part of the McHenry County, Illinois, fire and rescue disaster plan.

[6] Third and fifth alarms request, respectively, chief officer and 9 ambulance companies and chief officer and 15 ambulance companies.

Figure 2 — Accident scene

An estimated 90 fire and emergency response personnel and the McHenry County Coroner's Office responded and were directed by a paramedic triage officer to assist in the treatment and transportation of victims. Additionally, officers from 12 police departments responded and assisted with the accident investigation and traffic control. In less than 90 minutes from the time the collision occurred, all seriously injured passengers had been transported to one of seven nearby hospitals. Table 1 lists the injuries reported in this accident.

Survival Aspects

The school busdriver, who sustained minor injuries, was wearing the three-point lap/ shoulder belt available at the driver's seat. Two other lap belt restraints were available (in the right front seat); however, none of the bus passengers was restrained.

The seven fatally injured, as well as four seriously injured, passengers had been seated at the rear of the bus in rows 9 through 12. Four passengers seated in rows seven and eight were seriously injured. There were two seriously injured passengers in rows 2 and 5 on the left

side. Fourteen passengers with minor injuries and four uninjured passengers were seated in rows 1 through 6. (For bus occupant seating and injury distribution, see figure 3.)

According to witness statements, five passengers seated in rows 8 through 11 stood up before the collision. One passenger was standing at his seat in row 10 when the collision occurred. The other four had reportedly moved into the aisle and were attempting to move forward in the bus. They were found in the aisle near rows 6 and 7 after the accident. Four of the five passengers who stood sustained moderate to severe injuries and one passenger sustained minor injuries.

Medical and Pathological Information

The minor to moderately injured passengers, who were seated primarily in rows 1 through 8, sustained concussions, contusions, lacerations, abrasions, and fractures of the head and extremities. The severely injured passenger in row 5 sustained lung contusions, a skull fracture, and a brain injury. The seriously injured passenger in row 7 sustained a concussion, a skull fracture, and a contusion of his

Table 1 — Injuries*

TYPE	Busdriver	Bus Passengers	Traincrew	Train Passengers	TOTAL
Fatal	0	7	0	0	7
Serious	0	10	0	0	10
Minor	1	14	0	0	15
None	0	4	3	**120	127
TOTAL	1	35	3	120	159

* Based on the injury criteria of Title 49 *Code of Federal Regulations* (CFR) 830.2 of the International Civil Aviation Organization, which the Safety Board uses in accident reports for all transportation modes. (For an injury table based on the Abbreviated Injury Scale (AIS) of the Association for the Advancement of Automotive Medicine, see appendix B.) NOTE: Further references to injuries throughout the report are based on the AIS, except when referring to fatally injured passengers.

** The railroad company estimated the number of commuter passengers.

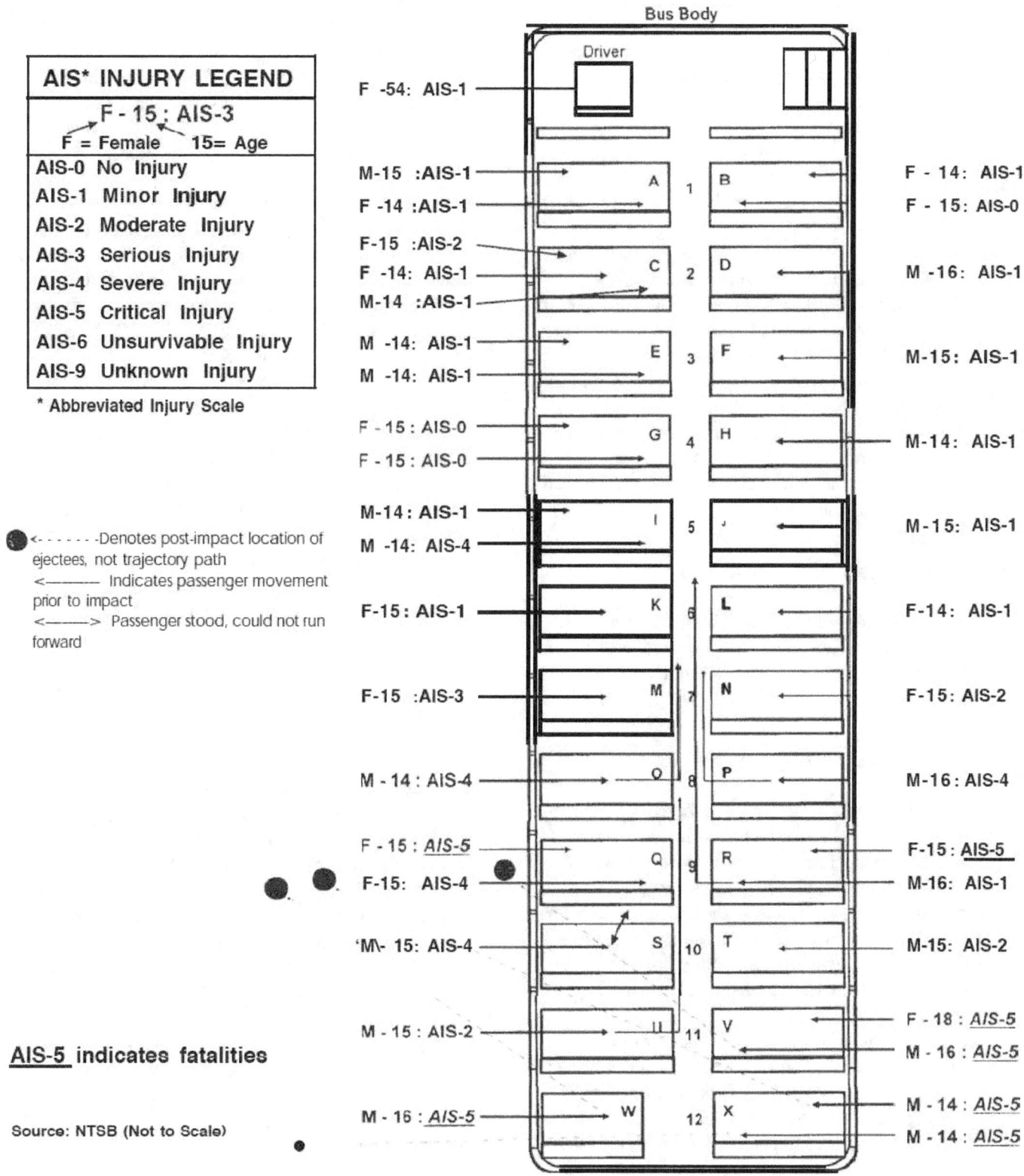

Figure 3 — School bus occupant seating and injury distribution diagram

spleen. The severely injured passengers seated in rows 8, 9, and 10 sustained multiple contusions, lacerations, and fractures of the head, shoulders, and extremities, and blunt trauma to the internal organs, such as the lungs, spleen, kidneys, and liver.

The fatally injured passengers, who were seated in rows 9, 11, and 12, sustained multiple fractures to the head and pelvis, and contusions and lacerations to the internal organs, such as the pancreas, liver, kidneys, spleen, and lungs. All seven of the fatally injured passengers sustained severe skull fractures (some with facial bone fractures) with subsequent massive brain injuries. A circular 0.2- to 0.5-inch abrasion was noted on the forehead of one fatally injured passenger and another had a 1.2- by 2-inch L-shaped abrasion on the left side of the head. The interior window frames and the perforated sound panels inside the school bus were shaped similarly to these abrasions.

Meteorological Information

At the time of the collision, according to the witnesses, the weather was clear and cold (temperature about 33 degrees Fahrenheit), the roadway was dry, and the sun was rising.

School Busdriver Information

The 54-year-old school busdriver had been hired by the TJA School District on August 1, 1983, as a secretary and bookkeeper. Between April 1986 and July 1989, she served as a bus dispatcher. She passed the Illinois written school busdriver examination at the State testing facility on January 2, 1987. She took the school bus road test at the facility three times between January 2 and 5, 1987, before passing it. After obtaining her Illinois school busdriver permit on January 5, 1987, which she has since renewed annually, she substituted, when necessary, for the regular busdrivers. She had a valid Illinois commercial driver license (CDL) with a passenger endorsement, which expires on March 22, 1997. When she took the CDL test on April 19, 1991, she passed the knowledge and passenger

tests; however, she failed the air brake test. The TJA School District thereupon submitted a letter to the Illinois Board of Education stating that she had been driving a school bus for over 2 years, which enabled her to be "grandfathered" and receive her CDL. She also possessed a valid Illinois driver license. Her driving record showed no traffic violations or convictions.

The busdriver was selected on July 15, 1989, for the new position of assistant transportation director for the TJA School District. Her duties included assisting the transportation director with planning school bus routes, interviewing and hiring new school busdrivers, and overseeing busdriver training. She supervised the State-certified school busdriver trainers. Although she was not certified as a trainer, she was responsible for auditing and evaluating the performance of 92 school busdrivers, including the substitute drivers, and for monitoring the performance of a secretary and 2 dispatchers. She also acted as liaison between the school busdrivers, the parents, and the school administration. Her personnel file contained many letters of appreciation for her work with the school district. No written evaluations of her performance from her supervisor were on file, either concerning administrative tasks or school bus operation.

Since 1976, the Illinois Operation Lifesaver program has provided instruction to increase public awareness of hazards at railroad/highway grade crossings and to develop proper driver behavioral patterns at these grade crossings. A Union Pacific Railroad Company (UP) representative had presented Operation Lifesaver material to school busdrivers in the TJA School District area on three occasions since 1988. Forty, 250, and 263 busdrivers participated at the presentations in 1988, 1989, and 1992, respectively. The busdriver who drove the accident bus had attended the 1992 Operation Lifesaver presentation. The training curriculum does not address short queuing areas such as that encountered in this accident.

Illinois requires school busdrivers to receive 4 to 8 hours of training by State-certified instructors who cover various subjects on school bus operation. The school busdriver completed this mandated initial training course on January 22, 1987. The annual renewing of her school busdriver permit required that she attend one 2-hour refresher course each year. The TJA School District provided 12 certification notices that she had attended State-mandated refresher courses between 1987 and 1995, and two of these courses, according to its records, were presented by Operation Lifesaver. The last refresher course that she attended before the accident was in June 1995 and covered the "stop, look, and listen" procedures to follow at railroad/highway grade crossings. In addition to the State-mandated courses, in July 1989, the busdriver attended and passed a workshop on advanced school bus driving maneuvers.

The busdriver reported that she was in good health. During her last work-related physical on January 16, 1995, her hearing was tested and found to be within the normal range. She wore glasses to improve her vision in both eyes to 20/20 and was wearing them at the time of the accident. The busdriver said that she suffered from sinus problems during the winter. She stated that she had taken an over-the-counter medicine (Equate Suphedrine) on the morning of the day before the accident and one over-the-counter medicine (Equate cold decongestant) for a cold and sinus condition on the night before the accident.

Before the accident, the school busdriver and her husband had been on vacation for 6 days, returning at 9:30 p.m. on October 22, 1995, whereupon she went to bed between 10 and 10:30 p.m. On October 23, 1995, the busdriver awoke at her usual time, between 6:30 and 7 a.m. and went to work between 7:45 and 8 a.m. She drove a morning elementary school bus route, performed her office duties, left work at 5 p.m., attended a meeting, and went to bed between 10:30 and 11 p.m. She followed the same basic routine the next day. On the day of the accident, October 25, 1995, after sleeping about 7 hours 30 minutes, the driver woke about

6 a.m. and reported to work at 6:30 a.m. She had been awake for 1 hour 11 minutes and on duty for 41 minutes when the accident occurred.

The school busdriver stated that she had driven 21 of the 42 school days that year; she would drive mornings or afternoons and sometimes both. She reported that before the day of the accident, she had never driven either a school bus or a passenger car over the Algonquin Road grade crossing.

School Bus Information

The 1992 American Transportation Company (Am Tran) 71-passenger school bus had a Navistar chassis, a diesel engine, power steering, and an automatic transmission. Its gross vehicle weight rating was 29,000 pounds; when the accident occurred its estimated weight was 23,390 pounds. The odometer reading was 60,083. The school bus was approximately 8 feet wide, 10 feet high, 38 feet 4 inches long, and had a 276-inch wheel base.

The school bus had 12 rows of 3-passenger bench seats on the right side, and the first 11 rows of 3-passenger bench seats on the left side. The last row on the left side consisted of a 2-passenger bench seat. The bus was equipped with a three-point lap/shoulder belt (emergency-locking retractor) for the driver and two other restraints.[7] The bus had two emergency roof hatches.

The school bus was equipped with an AM/FM radio-cassette player and eight speakers. One speaker was above the driver's head and the remaining left side speakers were above the windows at rows 2, 8, and 11. The right side radio speakers were above the windows at rows 2, 5, 8, and 11. The bus was also equipped with a two-way radio and a paging system located in front of and over the driver's head. All interior

---

[7] These had been installed for the children of the regular school busdriver.

roof panels of the bus were perforated to attenuate interior noise levels.[8]

The only defect mentioned in the chassis manufacturer's records was the recall and repair of the bus's fuel tank cage. School bus maintenance records did not indicate any recurring problems with the bus, except for three alternator replacements in 1995. Safety Board investigators conducted a postaccident inspection of the school bus and found no mechanical defects.

School Bus Damage

The inward deformation of the left rear side of the school bus extended along the last 105 inches (8.75 feet) of the bus to a maximum of 40 inches at the left rear corner. Contact damage and light gray paint transfers were found at the left rear corner and extended 36 inches toward the front. The left rear tire was punctured and the same light gray paint transfer was found on the tire. (The train was painted light gray.) The rear frame members of the chassis were bent rightward (the direction the train was going) at approximately a 41-degree angle (with the left side chassis frame rail bent 82 inches). The left side floor had separated between rows 7 and 8. The bus body from the cowling rearward (just in front of the driver's position) had separated from the chassis during impact. The right side of the bus sustained buckling inward between rows 7 and 10, extending from the roof down the entire side wall. A 2 ½-inch-long scratch was found above the 10th window on the left side of the bus. A dent with a yellow paint transfer similar to the yellow paint on the traffic signal stanchion was above and to the right of the 10th window on the right side of the bus.

The windshield and eight of the left side windows were completely broken out, and the left side window frames were skewed and buckled. Although the right side window frames were bent inward and buckled, the glass in 10 of the 13 windows was intact. The right front entrance door had been torn from all but one of its front hinges and was lying partially inside the entranceway. The rear emergency roof hatch was dislodged. The rear emergency door had buckled severely and was partially open after the accident. Scrapes were found on the top and right side of the fuel tank; however, it was not punctured, nor was there any leakage.

The interior of the roof was deformed inward and upward in the rear. The left side seatbacks in rows 9 through 12 were displaced rearward. The right side seats in rows 8 through 12 were either warped, raised upward, displaced leftward, or missing seat cushions. The left side seat in row 12 was displaced inward 17 inches from the sidewall to the center of the bus.

The transmission gear selector was found locked in the "drive" position. The upper part of the steering wheel was gouged and bent to the right. The driver's side window was found open 3/8 inch. The radio control volume was found on and turned up slightly more than ¼ of a turn. The clearance and dome light switches were in the "on" position. The front heat and auxiliary heat switches were in the "low" position.

Train Information

Train 624, owned by METRA and operated by the UP, was transporting passengers from the suburbs into Chicago. It consisted of a bilevel cab control car,[9] 6 bilevel passenger cars, and a locomotive. At the time of the accident, the locomotive was pushing the passenger cars from the rear and the train was being operated from the cab control car. The train length was 650 feet and its weight was 570 tons.

---

[8] The *Illinois Minimum Safety Standards for Construction of Type I School Buses* states in Section 4.2.17 that "thermal and acoustic materials shall be installed in the ceiling and the sides of the body to reduce heat transfer and the interior noise level."

[9] Cab control cars produce no tractive effort, but control train movements via train line electrical connections to the locomotive at the opposite end of the train. They contain the same passenger seating configuration as the other bilevel passenger cars.

The cab control car (no. 8751) had a body width of 10 feet (with handrails extending an additional 3 ½ inches on each side) and was equipped with a 97-channel radio and a WAB-CO two-chime whistle with two trumpets directed forward. The cab control car was equipped with a headlight and an orange rotating light, both of which were operating at the time of the accident. The leading face of the cab control car was striped with red and white reflectorized paint.

Train Damage

The front of the cab control car sustained 7 inches of maximum inward crush to the left side of the left collision post. Yellow paint transfers were on the left rear side sill step and the step was destroyed. The left end ladder and sill hand-hold were crushed. The speedometer cable sheathing was damaged on the left side at the first axle. The toilet drain pipe and water fill pipe housing were damaged on the left side. The left side sill step on the first passenger car was broken. The second passenger car sustained left side scrape marks. Postaccident inspection of the cab control car revealed no unusual precollision conditions.

Traincrew Information

METRA train 624 had three UP crew members, including the engineer, the conductor, and the trainman/collector. Neither the conductor nor the trainman/collector was in the cab control car when the accident occurred.

The 45-year-old train engineer had been hired by the Chicago and North Western Railway Company (C&NW) on October 9, 1973. He had worked as a machinist's helper and machinist until July 16, 1976, when he transferred to engine service. He was promoted to locomotive engineer on November 22, 1977, and has operated freight trains and METRA passenger trains since that time. He successfully completed his last locomotive engineer certification examination on September 1, 1995. He is qualified to operate over a territory of several subdivisions, including the Harvard subdivision in which the accident occurred.

The engineer works as an "extra board" engineer, filling in for regularly assigned engineers as the need arises. He had operated trains on the accident route since October 13, 1995, because the regular engineer was on extended leave due to illness. That assignment included operating several METRA commuter trains between Crystal Lake and Chicago.

The engineer said that he was in good health and was not ill, nor did he take any medication on the day of the accident. His last physical examination was on August 31, 1995. His vision was 20/30 in both eyes and his hearing tested within acceptable parameters. He was wearing safety sunglasses at the time of the accident.

The weekend before the accident, the engineer had been off duty and he spent his time painting his house. From Monday through Wednesday (the accident day), he worked his usual schedule, which involves operating four trains daily. He normally awakens about 4 or 4:15 a.m. and leaves for work at 5 a.m.; he commutes 1 hour and 20 minutes to work. He reports for duty at 6:30 a.m. and takes a METRA train from Crystal Lake into Chicago, arriving at about 8:30 a.m. Between 8:30 and 9:30 a.m., he takes the train to the coach yard for cleaning and the engine to another yard for refueling. He then eats breakfast and sleeps at a nearby facility for 4 hours. He reports back on duty at 3:15 p.m. and operates a train from Chicago to Winnetka, Illinois, arriving at approximately 6 p.m. He changes operating ends of the train and travels back to Chicago, arriving at about 6:30 p.m. He then is off duty from 6:30 p.m. to 7:30 p.m. (during which period he eats dinner) and goes back on duty, operating a train back to Crystal Lake, arriving at approximately 9 p.m. He goes off duty at 9:30 p.m. and travels the 1 hour and 20 minutes back home, arriving about 11 p.m. He eats a meal and falls asleep about 11:30 p.m.

On the accident day, he woke between 4:15 and 4:30 a.m. and arrived at work about 6:30 a.m. When the collision occurred, the engineer had been on duty for about 45 minutes and had been awake for about 3 hours, having had 5 hours sleep in his most recent sleep period, and 9 hours sleep in the previous 24 hours.

Toxicological Tests

Although not required by Federal regulation, the train engineer and the school busdriver complied with the Fox River Grove Police Department's request for blood and urine samples, which were analyzed at the Illinois State Police (ISP) laboratory in Maywood, Illinois. The Safety Board had portions of these samples sent to the Center for Human Toxicology (CHT) in Salt Lake City, Utah, for analysis.

The ISP toxicological analysis indicates that the school busdriver's blood and urine, obtained 4 hours after the accident, were negative for alcohol. The urine analysis detected acetaminophen, phenylpropanolamine, and pseudoephedrine. The CHT analysis of her urine sample detected caffeine, acetaminophen, pseudoephedrine, phenylpropanolamine, and chlorpheniramine. Her blood sample showed pseudoephedrine at a concentration of 36 nanograms per milliliter. No other drugs[10] were found in her blood.

Toxicological tests conducted by the ISP of the engineer's blood and the urine samples obtained 5 ½ hours after the accident were negative for alcohol and controlled substances. Additional CHT tests showed that his urine sample contained caffeine and no other drugs.

Operations Information

School District.—The school bus was owned and operated by TJA School District 47/155. In 1974, School District 47, which includes students from kindergarten through 8th grade, and

School District 155, which includes students from 9th through 12th grade, had entered into a Pupil Transportation Joint Agreement. At the time of the accident, the school district operated 72 buses varying in size from 12- to 78-passenger capacity. Average age of the vehicles was 6 years. The operation encompassed 2 counties, 99 percent in McHenry County and 1 percent in Lake County, with a total of 174 routes. About half of these school bus routes crossed railroad/highway grade crossings. The TJA School District had about 80 grade crossings.

The TJA director of transportation, hired in 1984, had previously been a school busdriver and later became a certified school busdriver instructor for the State. His staff includes an assistant director (the accident school busdriver), two dispatchers, and a secretary/bookkeeper. The director is responsible for monitoring and evaluating drivers, planning routes, and establishing school bus specifications.

The transportation director said that school district routes were planned and reviewed for new school passengers and for route hazards (dangerous or unsafe conditions, such as vegetation obscuring stop signs, work zones, etc.) during the summer and that he would himself drive the routes, sometimes in his car and other times in a school bus. He said that his office used a commuter train schedule and the school bus route schedule and coordinated them in an attempt to avoid scheduling crossings at times when train traffic might be present. He also stated that he relied on community input, driver input, and his own personal knowledge of the routes for hazard recognition. He said that upon receipt of a hazard report, his followup procedure would be to go out and personally look at the scene. He had not driven this particular bus route before the accident.

Drivers were supposed to report the hazards they encountered, either verbally or by making a note on their daily pretrip inspection form. After

---

[10] Amphetamines, barbiturates, benzodiazepine, cannabinoids, cocaine, opiates, phencyclidine, and metabolites of these drugs.

receiving the report, the director or his assistant would talk to the driver and make an appropriate note on the individual route sheet. Safety Board investigators examined the route maps provided to the drivers of the accident route and found no mention of any hazardous locations. The *TJA School District Handbook* called for route maps to be updated bimonthly and stated that drivers should review each map for any corrections, and initial and date the map to indicate accuracy.

The Illinois Vehicle Code 625 ILCS 5/11-1425 requires school busdrivers to:

Stop when traffic [is] obstructed. No driver shall enter an intersection or a marked crosswalk or drive onto any railroad grade crossing unless there is sufficient space on the other side of the intersection, crosswalk, or railroad grade crossing to accommodate the vehicle he is operating without obstructing the passage of other vehicles, pedestrians, or railroad trains notwithstanding any traffic-control signal indication to proceed.

The regular school busdriver, who had driven the route on which the accident occurred for the previous 5 years, had a total of 16 years of experience driving school buses. She stated that she usually gets to the crossing where the accident took place at 6:55 a.m. and does not encounter any trains. If the traffic signal at US 14 is red, she stays stopped south of the tracks until it changes to green before crossing the railroad tracks. She said that she did not know the size of the queuing area but felt safer staying on the south side of the tracks. She explained that if a car is in front of her waiting for the red light to change, she knows that there is not enough room for the bus to fit. If the traffic signal at US 14 is green as she approaches, she does her "stop, look, and listen" and remains stopped on the south side of the tracks because she knows that the light will turn red soon and she does not want to get stopped behind a car and fail to fit in the queuing area.

The regular substitute driver for this route also said he stops the bus on the south side of the crossing because he does not believe that a bus could safely fit into the queuing area. He proceeds across the tracks only on a new green signal cycle to avoid having to stop in the queuing area.

A school busdrivers from District 3 (that transports the kindergarten through 8th grade students)[11] stated that she crosses the tracks about six times a day in her personal vehicle and that before US 14 was widened in 1990, the storage area had been large enough to accommodate a car and a school bus. However, since the widening, a school bus has to drive onto the pedestrian crosswalk to fit. Therefore, she trains the other two school busdrivers in her district never to stop on the north side of the railroad tracks. She said that it is difficult to judge the rear of the school bus at that location because the queuing area is on a downgrade. The District 3 school busdrivers travel eastbound on US 14, and sometimes cross the tracks when the light is red (if no cars are in front of them) because they can make a right turn on red.

The TJA director of transportation is responsible for establishing bus specifications for school buses used in the school district. No written or verbal recommendations or policies address the use of radio equipment on the school buses. The director stated that radio equipment usage is at the discretion of the driver. He said that the radio-tape cassette stereo system was purchased as an information tool for the drivers to obtain weather and traffic reports. The two-way radio is used primarily for communication between the busdrivers and the dispatcher. He also explained that the radio pacifies the students. The public address system is an academic aid used on field trips when informational cassette tapes are played. A representative from a school bus manufacturer stated that about 40 percent of the school buses ordered in the

---

[11] District 3 is a completely separate organization and has only three drivers and six bus routes.

United States are equipped with radio-tape cassette players.

Railroad.—Movement of trains over this territory is governed by operating rules, timetable instructions, and signal indications of an automatic block signal system[12] supplemented by an intermittent automatic train stop system.[13] On April 25, 1995, the UP acquired the C&NW railroad; however, the railroad dispatching facility that monitors and controls train movements remained in Chicago. At the time of the accident, UP owned and maintained the tracks. Under a "purchase of service" agreement, UP crews operated and maintained the train equipment owned by METRA.

Train operations through Fox River Grove consist of 57 regularly scheduled METRA commuter trains and approximately 6 freight trains daily. The weekday morning commuter train service begins at 4:59 a.m. and ends at 8:09 a.m. Service consists of 13 eastbound trains and 1 westbound train. The maximum authorized speed is 70 mph for commuter/passenger trains and 50 mph for freight trains.

Description of the Accident Site

General.—The collision occurred on Algonquin Road near the intersection of US 14 in the Village of Fox River Grove, Illinois. Two railroad tracks cross Algonquin Road about 45 feet south of US 14. The railroad/highway grade crossing is "active," meaning it is equipped with gates, lights, and a bell.[14] US 14 is an arterial highway that passes through the village's business district. A commuter rail station is located adjacent to the intersection, and several busi-

nesses and a fire station are on Algonquin Road just south of the railroad tracks. Algonquin Road then winds through a residential area. (Refer to figure 1.) The 1993 average daily traffic count for US 14 was 26,300. The 1995 average daily traffic count for Algonquin Road was 5,282. No pedestrian counts had been made at the intersection before the accident.

U.S. Route 14.—US Route 14 is an east/west highway with a posted speed limit of 35 mph through the Village of Fox River Grove. The highway extends across the northern part of the state. Near the accident site, the highway consists of two westbound lanes and two eastbound lanes, separated by a center turn lane. A 6-foot-wide striped pedestrian crosswalk extends across US 14 east of Algonquin Road.

Algonquin Road.—Algonquin Road is a north/south village street that intersects and ends at US 14 and has a posted speed limit of 30 mph. The portion of street north of the railroad tracks consists of one southbound lane, one northbound 12-foot-wide lane, and a northbound 11-foot-wide lane (one left turn lane, and one through/right turn lane). The Village of Fox River Grove designated Algonquin Road a truck route and imposed size and weight restrictions on it.

Algonquin Road intersects the railroad tracks and US 14 at a 75-degree angle. Eighty feet south of the grade crossing, the northbound approach is a 2.5 percent upgrade that transitions to a 7.7 percent upgrade leading up to the grade crossing. Between the railroad tracks and US 14, the roadway slopes down 7.8 percent. The roadway is level 9 feet north of and 3 feet south of the outer rails. (See figures 4 and 5.)

In addition to the stop line and the pedestrian crosswalk mentioned above, traffic signals mounted on breakaway signal supports with pedestrian signal indicators were on the southeast, southwest, and northeast corners of the Algonquin Road/US 14 intersection. No stop line was on the south side of the tracks.

---

[12] The Association of American Railroads defines this as a series of consecutive blocks governed by block signals, cab signals, or both, actuated by a train, or engine, or by certain conditions affecting the use of a block.

[13] The Federal Railroad Administration defines this as a system so arranged that its operation will automatically result in the application of the brakes until the train has been brought to a stop.

[14] These are referred to throughout the report as "crossing warning devices."

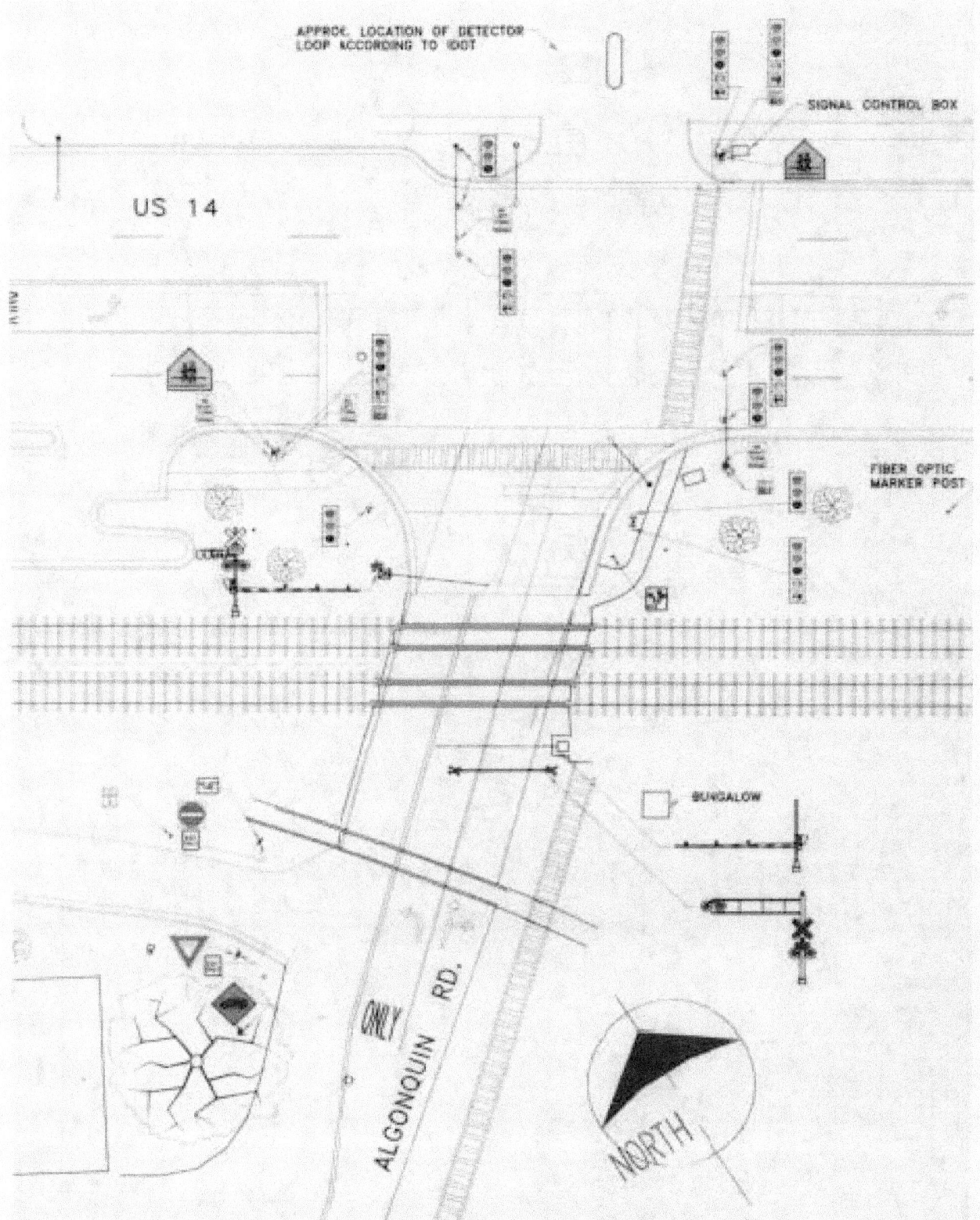

Figure 4 — Diagram of accident site (Courtesy of Safety Engineering Associates, Inc.)

16

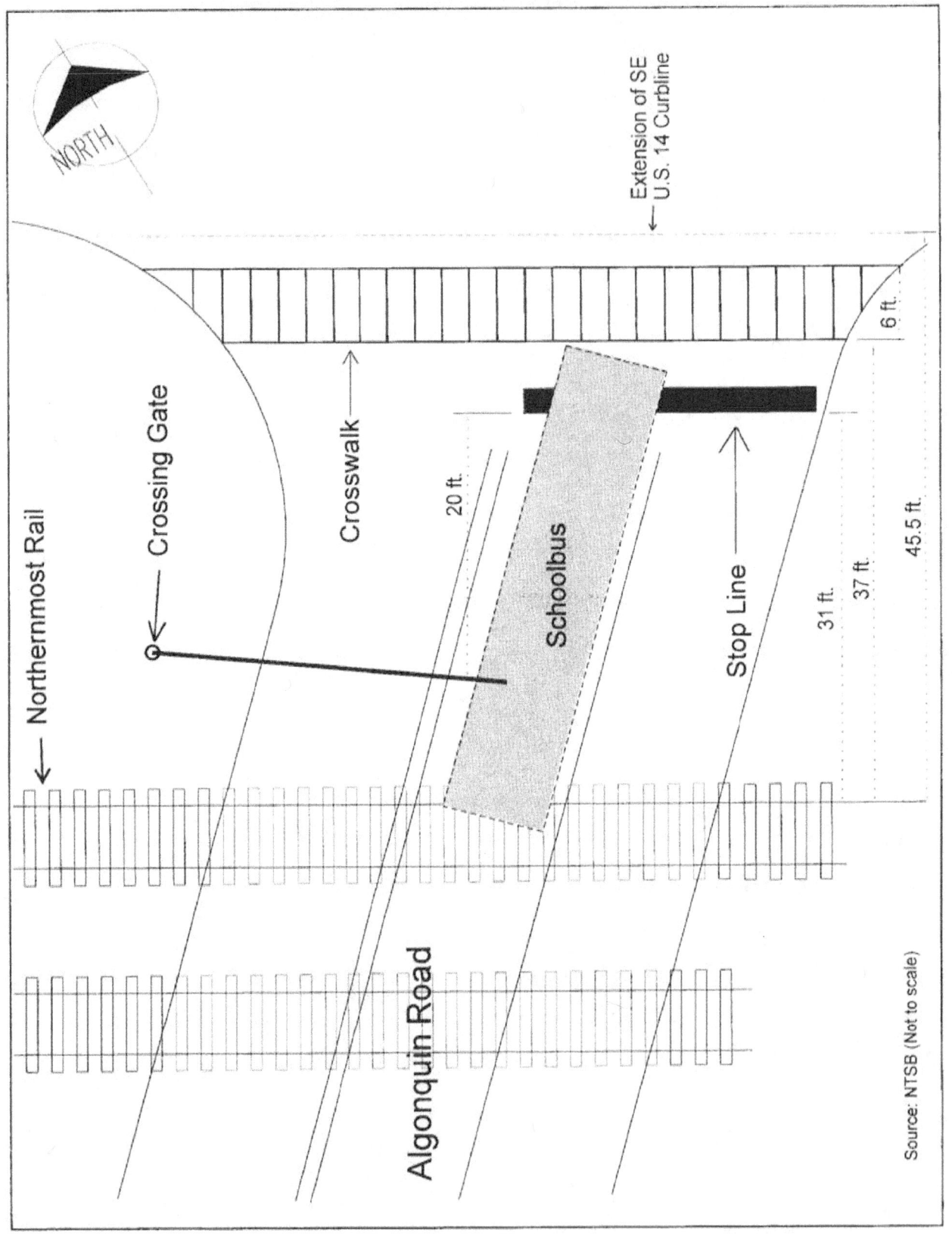

Figure 5 — Diagram of queuing area

Source: NTSB (Not to scale)

Algonquin Road Grade Crossing Accident History.—Safety Board investigators gathered accident information from data bases of three sources: the Fox River Grove Police Department, the UP, and the Federal Railroad Administration (FRA). The Fox River Grove Police Department records had the largest number of incident/accident reports for February 1990 through September 1995. These records indicated that during this period 20 accidents/incidents occurred, resulting in no fatalities or injuries (see table 2). Nineteen accidents/incidents involved vehicles striking or being struck by railroad gates; eleven involved commercial vehicles.

In the month before the accident, on September 18, 1995, a pickup truck driver drove northbound across the tracks after the crossing warning devices had been activated. The pickup truck's rear bumper extended over the railroad tracks and the driver drove forward to move off the tracks, striking the vehicle in front of him. An eastbound train then struck the rear bumper of the pickup truck.

Track.—The double main tracks are approximately 13 feet 6 inches from center to center. The accident occurred on the northern track. The track is standard gauge continuous welded rail, laid in 1982. The track geometry through the crossing is straight and level.

The UP designated the track to meet FRA Class 4 requirements and maintained it to meet the track safety standards for this designation. This class of track allows a maximum operating speed of 60 mph for freight trains and 80 mph for passenger trains. A review of the track inspection records revealed no anomalies.

Grade Crossing Traffic Controls.—The grade crossing inventory number is U.S. Department of Transportation (DOT)/FRA 176 958L. Both approaches were posted with a sign indicating that two railroad tracks were at the railroad crossing. The crossing was also equipped with flashing lights, a bell, and two red and white striped crossing gates, each with three round, 4-inch-diameter lights attached. Sixteen round, 12-inch-diameter, flashing lights were mounted on the signal masts and the cantilever.[15] The cantilever was located on the south side of the railroad tracks. Although Federal regulations require advance railroad pavement markings at active grade crossings, the site had none.

Railroad Signal System

The railroad grade crossing signal system uses a microprocessor to calculate the speed of the train and the time it will take for the train to arrive at the crossing. The system activates the crossing warning devices at a predetermined constant warning time regardless of the train's speed. A constant warning time device, as defined by the Association of American Railroads (AAR), provides a relatively uniform warning time. This time will fluctuate somewhat due to variances in the train speed and lump impedance[16] levels due to environmental, ballast, and track conditions. The amount of warning time is limited by the length of the approach circuit to the grade crossing and the maximum speed of the train approaching the crossing.

After a train enters an approach circuit, the microprocessor takes approximately 4 seconds (according to the operations manual) to measure the rate of change in the circuit voltage, electric current levels, and signal phase relationships, and to calculate the train's speed. The system then determines the point in time (depending on the train's speed and its distance from the crossing) at which to activate the crossing warning devices to provide the desired advance warning time.

---

[15] Defined by the Association of American Railroads as "a structure consisting of a ground mast and a horizontal arm extending to one side, used to support one or more signals as required for multiple tracks, or one or more highway grade crossing signals."

[16] The tendency to impede the flow of current in a manner similar to resistance.

18

Table 2 — Accidents on Algonquin Road

Date of Accident	Description of Accident
5/13/90	Driver of a northbound vehicle is blinded by sun and strikes gate.
2/01/90	After waiting for one train to clear, a northbound vehicle proceeds across tracks only to have an approaching train reactivate the gate, which lowers and strikes the vehicle.
9/13/90	Driver of a southbound truck strikes gate and keeps going (hit and run).
9/15/90	Driver of a northbound vehicle strikes gate and keeps going (hit and run).
1/21/91	A southbound tractor trailer strikes gate.
5/08/91	As a southbound mixing truck is crossing tracks, the gate lowers between the cab and the mixer and is broken off.
5/22/91	As a southbound van proceeds across tracks, the gate lowers, striking the vehicle, and is broken.
6/25/91	As a northbound tractor trailer is waiting to turn left, the gate lowers, striking the vehicle, and is broken.
7/06/91	As a northbound van proceeds across tracks, the gate lowers, striking the vehicle, and is broken.
7/25/91	Car northbound on Algonquin Road strikes gate and keeps going (hit and run).
8/16/91	As the gate begins to raise, a plumbing truck begins moving and clips the gate.
10/25/93	As a truck northbound on Algonquin Road proceeds across tracks, the gate lowers, striking the vehicle, and is broken.
1/24/94	As a truck northbound on Algonquin Road proceeds across tracks, the gate lowers, striking the vehicle, and is broken.
7/25/94	As a tractor trailer is making a southbound turn from US 14 and is proceeding across the tracks, the gate lowers, strikes the vehicle, and is damaged.
11/23/94	Driver of a southbound dump truck crashes through lowered gates. Driver is subsequently charged with DUI.
12/13/94	Northbound vehicle that is stopped on the tracks backs into gate.
1/31/95	A vehicle rear-ends another vehicle on US 14.
5/05/95	Large southbound tractor trailer strikes gate.
5/08/95	Vehicle southbound on Algonquin Road strikes gate.
9/18/95	Two vehicles northbound on Algonquin are stopped in the queue area for a red light at US 14 when railroad lights activate. Driver of second vehicle moves forward to pull away from tracks and strikes front vehicle.

Although the microprocessor continues to monitor and calculate the train's speed and distance to the crossing to allow for trains of varying speeds, once the signal is sent to activate the crossing warning devices, the warning time cannot be changed. If a train accelerates, decelerates, or brakes after the crossing warning devices have been activated, the train may take more or less time to arrive at the crossing than originally calculated.

The desired advance warning time for a crossing signal controlled by such a microprocessor is entered into the unit by adjusting its warning time switch, which is known as a "thumbwheel." During the 5 years before the accident, the thumbwheel on the microprocessor at the accident site had been set at 30 seconds for the northernmost railroad track and the narrow band shunt was connected to the rails approximately 3,053 feet from the edge of the crossing (or 3,080 feet to the center of the crossing). However, 2 weeks before the accident (October 11, 1995), the thumbwheel was reset at 25 seconds. According to the UP, the thumbwheel setting was changed to 25 seconds to ensure consistency at that crossing and throughout the railroad's property. UP officials stated that the thumbwheel setting change did not change the minimum constant warning time of 20 seconds. Should any malfunction occur, the microprocessor is programmed to activate the crossing warning devices immediately.

FRA regulations address required minimum warning time in Title 49 *CFR*, Part 234.225, "Activation of Warning System," which states:

A highway/rail grade crossing warning system shall be maintained to activate in accordance with the design of the warning system, but in no event shall it provide less than 20 seconds warning time before the grade crossing is occupied by rail traffic.

The State of Illinois Requirements for Highway Grade Crossing Protection, Section VII, "Operating Time," states:

All protection devices shall indicate the approach of a train for not less than twenty (20) seconds before the arrival at the crossing of the fastest train operated over the crossing.

Title 92: Transportation; Chapter III: Illinois Commerce Commission; Subchapter C: Rail Carriers; Part 1535: Crossings of Rail Carriers and Highways: Subpart C: *Establishment, Construction, and Maintenance of Grade Crossings*, at 1535.350, "Circuits," states:

Automatic flashing light signals shall be arranged to indicate the approach of trains on all main tracks and on auxiliary tracks included between the signals where the speed of trains approaching the crossing exceeds 5 mph, for not less than 20 seconds before the arrival at the crossing of the fastest train over the track.

The AAR, in its *Recommended Practices: Part 3.3.10, Recommended Instructions for Calculating Approach Warning Times for Railroad Activated Highway Grade Crossing Warning Devices Minimum Warning Time* states: "Warning devices shall operate for a minimum of 20 seconds before a train enters the crossing."

The *Federal Highway Administration (FHWA) Railroad/Highway Grade Crossing Handbook* states:

On tracks where trains operate at speeds of 20 mph or higher, the circuits controlling automatic flashing light signals shall provide for a minimum operation of 20 seconds before the arrival of any train. This 20-second warning time is a MINIMUM (p.126).

A UP representative testified at the Safety Board's public hearing in January 1996 that:

We design our circuits for 25 seconds to give a 5-second buffer...because there are conditions out on the track that make us unable to give an exact warning time. These conditions are beyond our control, and we know that this warning time is going to fluctuate; so we put in a 5-second buffer to this 20 seconds.

He also stated:

...constant warning is more of a generic term, and these boxes are not capable of giving an exact constant warning for every train coming toward the crossing. There are too many variables in the condition of the soil, the traffic, etc., the different types of train movements toward the crossing. Some of them stop at platforms to pick up passengers, increasing speed, decreasing speed. So there is no way this box can give an exact warning for every train. But they do process the information to try to develop that time as close as possible.

The system, as designed, would provide a maximum of 25 seconds before the train reached the crossing in the case of a 70-mph train traveling at a constant speed (about 103 feet per second) crossing over an approach circuit located 3,080 feet[17] from the crossing with a thumbwheel setting of 30 seconds. In the same situation, with a thumbwheel setting at 25 seconds, the train would reach the crossing in about 24 seconds, a 1-second difference.

In the case of a 50-mph train traveling at a constant speed (73 feet per second) and a thumbwheel setting of 30 seconds, the microprocessor would delay activation of the crossing warning devices for about 12 seconds until the train traveled closer to the crossing, providing about 29 seconds of warning time. In the same situation, with a thumbwheel setting at 25 seconds, the microprocessor would delay activation of the crossing warning devices for about 17 seconds until the train traveled closer

to the crossing, providing about 24 seconds of warning time. (See figures 6 and 7.)[18]

When the signal is sent to the crossing warning devices, the flashing lights activate at the grade crossing and within 3 seconds, the gates begin to descend. Federal regulations Title 49 *CFR* Part 234.223 state:

Each gate arm shall start its downward motion not less than three seconds after flashing lights begin to operate and shall assume the horizontal position at least five seconds before the arrival of any train at the crossing.

At the accident crossing, once the microprocessor activates the crossing warning devices, the highway signal system is simultaneously sent a signal. This arrangement is known as a "highway interconnect circuit," which is a normally closed circuit (containing a flow of electrical current) that is broken when the electrical current is interrupted, giving an indication to the traffic signal system that the crossing warning devices have been activated. The highway signal system then immediately begins its railroad preempt sequence.[19] (As the rail signal system is very complex, more detail concerning it can be found in appendix C.)

History of Algonquin Road

Before 1989, US 14 was a two-lane, two-way roadway. Traffic on Algonquin Road had been controlled with a stop sign, and the area north of the railroad tracks (between the US 14 curb line and the northern rail) was about 80

---

[17] This is the approach circuit length measured by the railroad from the narrow band shunt to the middle of Algonquin Road.

[18] A lag time of about 8/10 second elapses before the grade crossing signal is activated, meaning a thumbwheel setting of 30 seconds at 3,080 feet produces 25 seconds rather than 26 seconds of railroad signal operation. A thumbwheel setting of 25 seconds actually produces 24 seconds. (See Tests and Research Section.)

[19] The highway traffic signal sequence that begins at the time the interconnect circuit is de-energized.

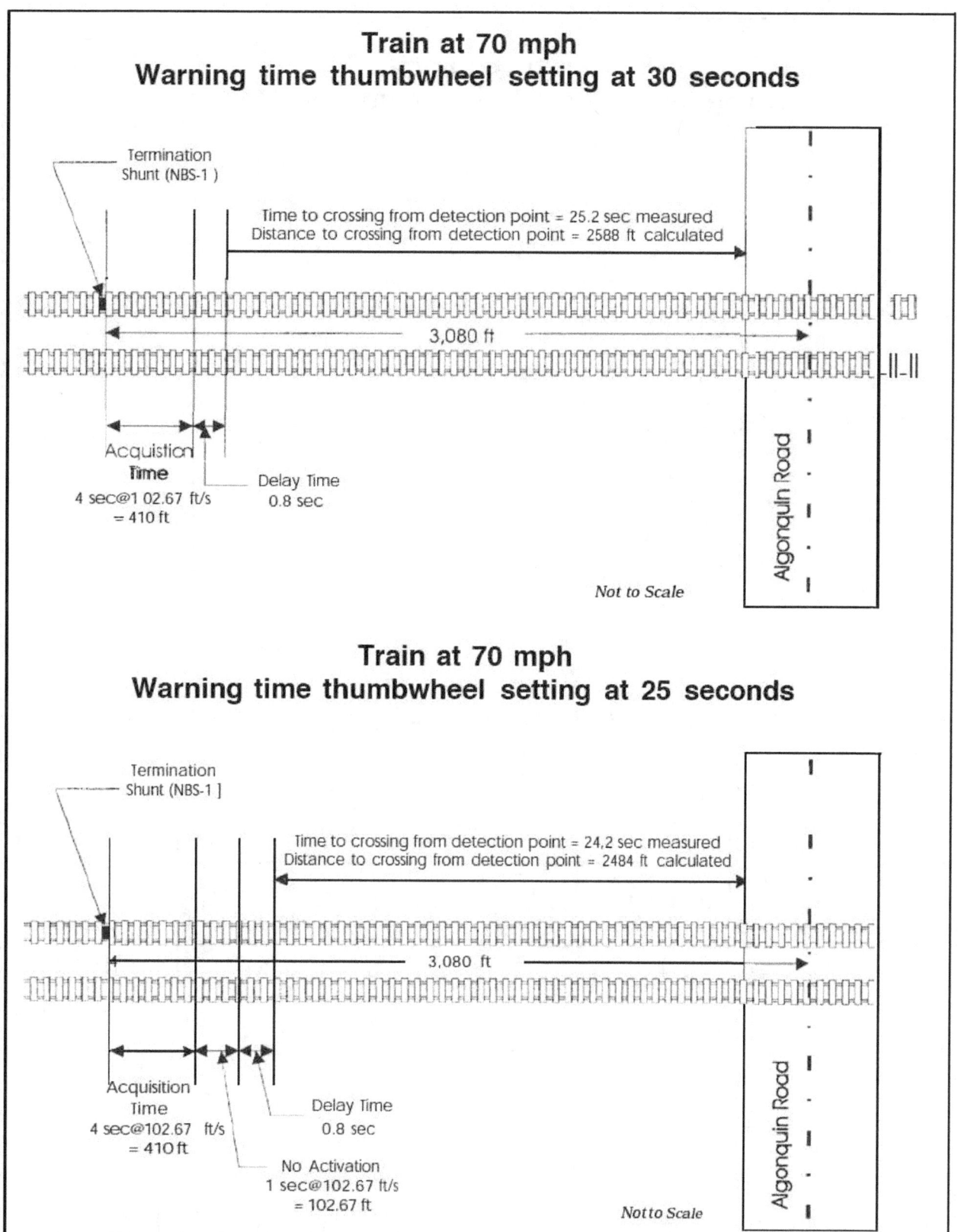

Figure 6 – Warning times for train at 70 mph

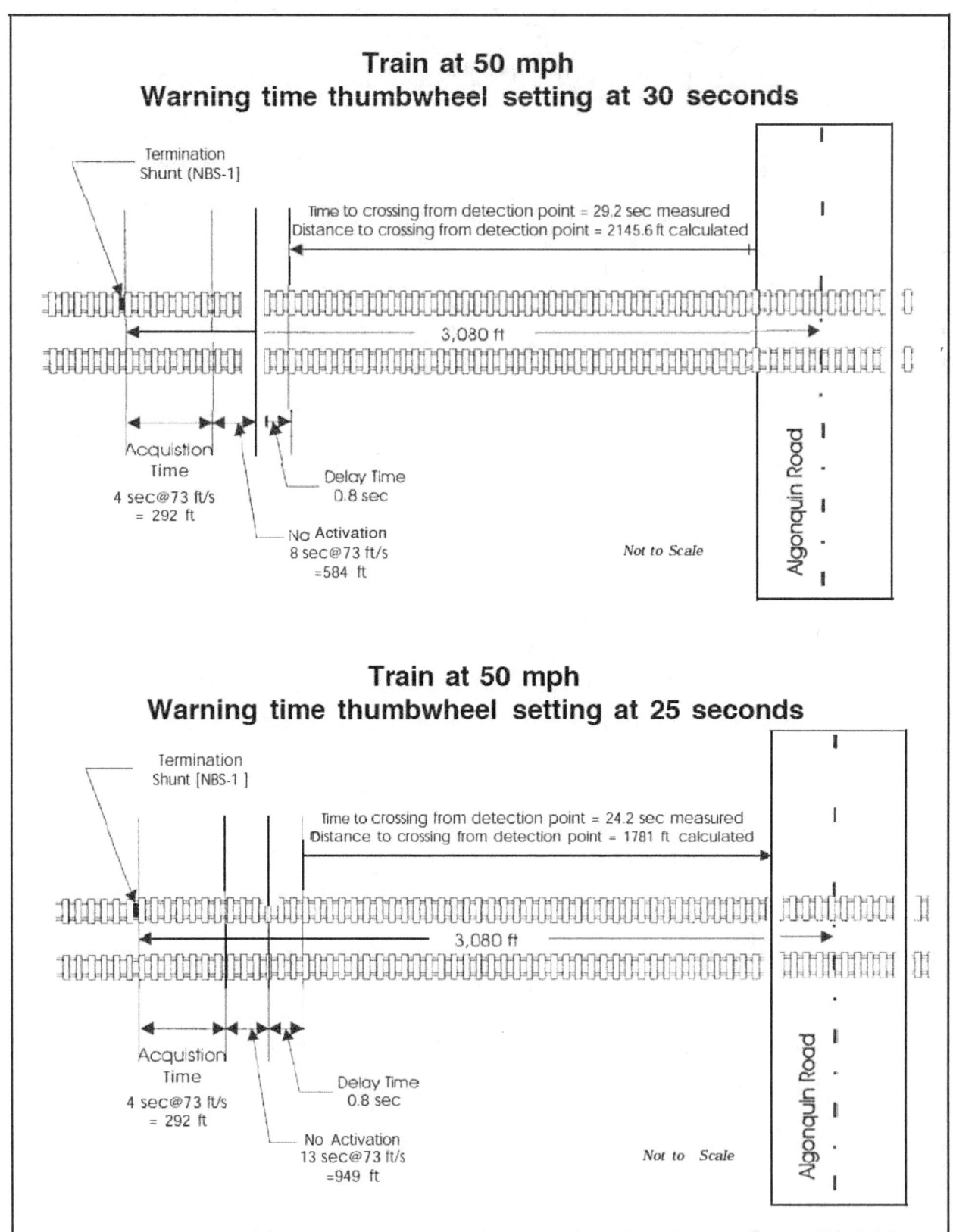

Figure 7 — Warning times for train at 50 mph

feet long. In 1989, IDOT widened US 14 using about 35 feet of railroad property, thereby shortening this area to about 45 feet. In addition, IDOT widened the Algonquin Road approach to the intersection from a two-lane to a three-lane roadway, adding a left turn lane for northbound traffic.

During the road-widening planning stages, the railroad expressed safety concerns to IDOT and local communities about US 14 being less than 50 feet from its railroad tracks. However, IDOT completed the road-widening as planned. The railroad/highway grade crossing on Algonquin Road had had mast-mounted flashing lights, crossing gates, and a bell. Renovations included adding a cantilever with flashing lights at the grade crossing and replacing the stop signs on Algonquin Road at US 14 with traffic signals. (See upcoming section addressing communication for more information.)

Highway Signal System

In conjunction with the road-widening project, the Algonquin Road/US 14 intersection was equipped with a traffic signal system. A highway traffic signal system alternately assigns the right-of-way to different traffic movements at an intersection. A traffic-actuated controller changes the signal indications (green, yellow, red). The signal indications in traffic-actuated controllers assign the right-of-way in response to variations in the level and speed of traffic, and when vehicle volumes vary over the course of the day. The accident intersection was equipped with roadway loop detectors to detect these variations in traffic levels.

The IDOT designed and installed a computerized traffic signal system using a master controller to coordinate the traffic movement on US 14. The plan was to use the master controller to synchronize and coordinate individual signal controllers at three adjacent intersections, US 14 at Lincoln Avenue, Algonquin Road, and State Route 22. However, once the equipment was installed, IDOT was unable to coordinate the traffic phases of the three intersections with the master controller, and the three signal controllers operated in an uncoordinated mode for about 5 years.

When installed in 1990, the traffic signal system at Algonquin Road was programmed with six separate traffic phases and two separate pedestrian phases. The crosswalk pedestrian phase across Algonquin Road was programmed to automatically display a pedestrian "Walk" indication with every green indication for US 14 between 5:45 a.m. and 10 p.m. on weekdays. In addition, if a railroad preempt call was received, the same pedestrian phase was displayed. Between 10 p.m. and 5:45 a.m. on weekdays and during the weekends, the "Walk" display for Algonquin Road appeared only when activated by the pedestrian push-button.

However, because IDOT was unable to coordinate the traffic phases through the master controller between January 1990 and October 1994, the traffic signal controller at Algonquin Road gave a pedestrian "Walk" indication only upon activation of a push-button located on the traffic signal support at the intersection. The automatic pedestrian phase never operated during this period. Because it was installed near a railroad crossing, the Algonquin Road highway signal system was also designed with a railroad preemption[20] sequence, and it was necessary to coordinate the railroad and the highway signal systems. In this case, the highway signals were interconnected with the railroad signals at the railroad signal box. The railroad system would signal the highway system, notifying it of the approach of a train. The highway signal system then would begin its preemptive sequence to allow time for vehicles and pedestrians to clear the railroad tracks.

Between January 1990 and October 1994, if a train approached while US 14 had a green indication, the US 14 signal would change to

---

[20] The transfer of the normal control of signals to a special signal control mode.

yellow for 4.5 seconds, and then to red for 1.5 seconds, and then the northbound Algonquin Road signal would change to a green indication. The sequence would allow 6 seconds to elapse before a green indication was displayed for northbound Algonquin Road, unless the pedestrian button had been pushed. Had a pedestrian pushed the button, the 12-second pedestrian phase would have been displayed, allowing 18 seconds to elapse before a green indication for northbound Algonquin Road was displayed.

In October 1994, new signal controllers were installed at the three intersections and a new master controller was installed and the equipment operated in a coordinated mode. At the time of the accident, the following railroad preemption sequence was programmed into the highway signal system if a train approached while US 14 had a green signal indication and the pedestrians crossing Algonquin Road had a "Walk" indication:

1. A flashing "Don't Walk" would display for 12 seconds for Algonquin Road pedestrians;

2. US 14 green indication would change to yellow for 4.5 seconds, with a solid "Don't Walk" indication for Algonquin Road;

3. US 14 yellow indication would change to red for 1.5 seconds;

4. Algonquin Road red indication would change to green for 12 seconds.

After the traffic signal system began operating in a coordinated mode, the preemption sequence included the automatic 12-second pedestrian clearance phase, thereby allowing 18 seconds to elapse before a green indication was presented to northbound Algonquin Road to clear traffic from the railroad tracks during a railroad preemption. (As the traffic signal system is very complex, more detail concerning it can be found in appendix D.)

Testimony from IDOT's contractors indicated that the preemption sequence could take as long as 21 seconds to reach a green indication for Algonquin Road under certain circumstances. For example, if a railroad preemption sequence occurred within 3 seconds of US 14 receiving a green indication, a 3-second delay would occur during the preemption sequence. This delay was programmed into the traffic signal sequence to prevent motorists on US 14 from receiving a momentary green indication.

The *Manual on Uniform Traffic Control Devices for Streets and Highways* (MUTCD)[21] and the *Railroad-Highway Grade Crossing Handbook*[22] provide specific standards, guidance, and recommendations for safely controlling traffic at intersections. The MUTCD was adopted as the official manual for the State of Illinois in 1990. The 1988 edition of the manual addresses the design and implementation of highway signal systems at railroad/highway grade crossings in Part 8C-6, "Traffic Signals At Or Near Grade Crossings," which states:

> When highway intersection traffic control signals are within 200 feet of a grade crossing, control of the traffic flow should be designed to provide the vehicle operators using the crossing a measure of safety at least equal to that which existed prior to the installation of such signals. Accordingly, design, installation, and operation should be based upon a total systems approach in order that all relevant features may be considered.

---

[21] The national standard governing traffic control devices on streets or highways placed there by the authority of a public body or official having jurisdiction to regulate, warn, or guide traffic. Published by the U.S. Department of Transportation, Federal Highway Administration, 1988.

[22] A handbook provided and sponsored by the U.S. Department of Transportation, Federal Highway Administration, to provide general information on railroad/highway grade crossings, FHWA TS-86-215, September 1986.

The MUTCD also provides directions for designing a preemption sequence for traffic signals to emphasize the importance of reaching a clearing green indication for the affected roadway as soon as possible. Under Part 8C-6, the MUTCD states:

> The preemption sequence initiated when the train first enters the approach circuit, shall at once bring into effect a highway signal display which will permit traffic to clear the tracks before the train reaches the crossing. The preemption shall not cause any short vehicular clearances and all necessary vehicular clearances shall be provided. However, because of the relative hazards involved, pedestrian clearances may be abbreviated in order to provide the track clearance display as early as possible.

Under 8C-5, "Train Detection," the MUTCD states:

> On tracks where trains operate at speeds of 20 mph or higher, circuits controlling automatic flashing light signals shall provide for a minimum operation of 20 seconds before arrival of any train on such track.

Under 8D-1 "Selection of Systems and Devices," the MUTCD states "Before a new or modified grade crossing traffic control system is installed, approval is required from the appropriate agency within a given state."

Regarding traffic signals, the *Railroad-Highway Grade Crossing Handbook* states:[23]

> Highway traffic control signals located at intersections within 200 feet of a crossing should be preempted by the approach of a train. Signals at intersections further than 200 feet from a crossing should also be preempted if traffic flow is such that vehicles queue up on the crossing, or if an engineering study determines the need for preemption. Railroad-highway grade crossing signals are coordinated with adjacent highway traffic control signals so that the operation of these separate control devices will at all times complement rather than negate each other.... A primary criterion is to avoid the entrapment of vehicles on the crossing by conflicting aspects of the highway signal and the crossing signal. The best way to do this is to prevent vehicle queues onto the tracks by the proper design and operation of the dual signal systems.

Regarding warning time, the *Railroad-Highway Grade Crossing Handbook* states:

> This 20 second warning time is a MINIMUM. The warning time should be of sufficient length to ensure clearance of a vehicle that might have stopped at the crossing and then proceeded to cross just before the flashing lights begin operation. Some railroads use a warning time of 25 seconds at crossings with automatic gates....

> Care should be taken to ensure that the warning time is not excessive....

> Excessive warning time has been determined to be a contributing factor in some accidents....

The *IDOT Traffic Signal Plan Preparation - A Design Guideline*, Section 2.2.5 Railroad Preemption Sequencing, published in November 1988, states, "Pedestrian clearances should coincide with vehicular clearances during railroad preemption to insure maximum track clearance." This section also states, "The designer shall document the review of his sequence with the railroad involved and send the District 1 Bureau of Traffic copies of this correspondence."

---

[23] U.S. Department of Transportation, Federal Highway Administration, September 1986, chapter IV, page 115.

The Illinois *Requirements for Railroad-Highway Grade Crossing Protection*, published in November 27, 1974, in Section VII, "Operating Time," states:

> All protection devices shall indicate the approach of a train for not less than 20 seconds before arrival at the crossing of the fastest train operated over the crossing. Local conditions may require a longer operating time. However, too long an indication by slow trains on high speed railroads is undesirable and suitable arrangements shall be made to compensate for differences in speeds of trains.

Railroad/Highway Signal Interaction

The Federal Highway Administration (FHWA) funded a February 1991 report[24] by the University of Tennessee that evaluated motorist responses, warning time expectations, and tolerance levels at three active railroad/ highway grade crossings with relatively high train and vehicular traffic volumes. The actions of 3,500 motorists were assessed during 445 train crossings. Research[25] indicates that extremely short warning times can be dangerous and

> Leave little margin of safety and poorly accommodate larger vehicles such as combination trucks and buses, especially if those vehicles must first come to a stop as required by many state laws.

The study also found that excessively long warning times (exceeding 40 seconds at flashing light signal crossings and 60 seconds at gated crossings) can cause drivers to lose confidence

in the traffic control system. Most motorists expect a train to arrive within 20 seconds of the traffic control device activating. Warning times in excess of 30 to 40 seconds caused many motorists to engage in risky crossing behavior.

The FRA requires railroads to provide a minimum of 20 seconds of warning time before train arrival at a grade crossing.[26] The circuitry can impart even more time than this, depending on the speed of the train (whether accelerating or decelerating) and the track condition.

Documentation and Communication Between IDOT and the Railroad

Between the construction project planning stages and the accident, IDOT, its consultants and contractors, and the railroads exchanged numerous documents that included information on the railroad and highway traffic signal systems. Additionally, representatives of these agencies and the Fox River Grove police responded to the Lincoln Avenue and Algonquin Road and US 14 intersections and the grade crossings for accidents and complaints at the intersection. The following is a chronological description of events related to the highway signal system timing.

On May 13, 1987, before the road-widening, the Illinois Commerce Commission had approved the construction plans for a railroad grade crossing at Foxmoor Road and the upgrading of the d.c. signal circuits at Algonquin Road and Lincoln Avenue. On August 4, 1987, the C&NW sent IDOT the design plans (dated July 6, 1987) for the Algonquin Road/US 14 intersection indicating that the railroad grade crossing approach circuit lengths for eastbound and westbound trains were "3,080 feet, 30 seconds at 70 mph." At that time, no highway traffic signals existed or were proposed at Algonquin Road.

---

[24] Stephen H. Richards, R.A. Margiotta, and G.A. Evans, *Warning Time Requirements at Railroad-Highway Grade Crossings with Active Traffic Control*, Report No. FHWA-SA-91-007, 1991.

[25] Stephen H. Richards and K.W. Heathington, *Assessment of Warning Time Needs at Railroad-Highway Grade Crossings with Active Traffic Control*, Transportation Research Record No. 1254, Traffic Control Devices for Highways, Work Zones, and Railroad Crossings, 1990.

[26] 49 *CFR* Part 234.225, "Activation of Warning System." Revised October 1, 1995.

On December 20, 1988, IDOT and the C&NW entered into an agreement related to the US 14 road-widening project and stipulated in the agreement that the grade crossing would conform to the *State Requirements for Railroad-Highway Grade Crossing Protection*, which called for 20 seconds advance warning time before rail traffic occupies the grade crossing. The specifications stated that long operating times were "undesirable" and that "suitable arrangements shall be made to compensate for differences in speeds of trains." The agreement discussed road-widening details, parking lot adjustments, and whether to install supplemental cantilever railroad signals at both Lincoln Avenue and Algonquin Road. It made no mention of the installation of highway traffic signals at Algonquin Road with an interconnect.

The IDOT hired a consultant to design the traffic signals in accordance with its specifications. The design plans, which included highway traffic signals at Algonquin Road, were approved by IDOT and a construction permit was issued. An internal IDOT memorandum dated November 20, 1989, indicated that on November 14, 1989, a C&NW representative discussed interconnection and preemption signal options with IDOT. In a November 21, 1989, letter[27] to the C&NW, IDOT states:

> Please note that at Lincoln Avenue, railroad interconnection currently exists. We would not anticipate major adjustments will be required at this location.

> At Algonquin Road, new signals are being installed. Please proceed with installation of relays as required to permit completion of interconnection at this location.

This letter also included the traffic signal sequence of operation diagram.

---

[27] Note: IDOT subsequently advised the Safety Board that the two roadways in this document -- Lincoln Avenue and Algonquin Road -- were reversed in the text.

In January 1990, the highway traffic signal system was installed at Algonquin and US 14. The IDOT engineering technician could not specifically recall nor does he have any documentation on how he programmed the traffic signals in January 1990. However, he stated in an interview with Safety Board investigators that when he is installing and turning on a traffic signal, he refers to the intersection plans for the signal installation that consist of a plan view of the intersection, the location of the signal facilities, the wiring diagram, and a sequence-of-operation program. He said that he would set the traffic signal timing for the normal sequence of operation and for any applicable railroad or emergency preemption sequences of operation. He would check the loop detectors using a loop analyzer, observe the traffic lights through a short cycle, test the conflict monitor by causing conflicting displays, and then place the signals in the normal operation position and conduct a physical inspection of the installation.

He stated that the pedestrian clearance time was calculated using the MUTCD guidelines and that a 12-second display of the Algonquin Road pedestrian indication of "Don't Walk" was programmed into the traffic signal sequence. He based his 12-second pedestrian phase on calculations using the width of Algonquin Road and the 4-feet-per-second pedestrian walking rate prescribed by the MUTCD.

The IDOT's engineering technician stated that in those cases when a preemption is programmed into the traffic signal system, he would test the preemption by having a railroad employee put in a simulated preemption call. When asked how the timing for the preemptive phase was determined, he said that he would use the same values for the yellow (4.5 seconds) and the all red (1.5 seconds) indications as in the normal sequence of operation. Then he would watch the grade crossing and, when the gates came down, make sure that the signal was green to clear the tracks and that an adequate amount of time was provided for traffic to get off the tracks and out of the intersection.

When asked how much information about the warning time did the railroad provide IDOT when a signal is turned on, the engineering technician responded, "You don't get any written documents...if we inquired, they [the railroad] could give us an answer...." He said that IDOT does not control the warning time duration and that to find out what the timing was,

We would establish some timing and put in some test calls and we could observe how long it was from the time we received the call from the railroad until their gates were horizontal and adjust our timing on that basis.

He stated that IDOT does not have a document indicating the values (including the railroad warning time) used when a signal is turned on.

In April 1991, the C&NW submitted construction prints to IDOT that indicated an approach warning time for track #1 (southern track) of 25 seconds and an approach warning time for track #2 (northern track) of 30 seconds. A footnote on the plan indicates "crossing to have 25 seconds of warning time." In a July 9, 1991, letter, the C&NW provided IDOT with another set of construction prints that states, "crossing to have 25 seconds of warning time."

On May 11, 1992, the C&NW provided IDOT and the Illinois Commerce Commission with a "project completion report" for relocating a crossing gate and installing a cantilever at the crossing. The report lists inspections and tests made during the project. The railroad indicated "yes" to the question "Do all approach start distances provide a minimum operation of 20 seconds before arrival of any train?"

In October 1994, IDOT replaced the master controller and the controllers at the three adjacent intersections.

In January 1995, IDOT's previous contractor installed an emergency vehicle preemption phase. This preemption phase is activated once an emergency vehicle call is received in the

traffic signal controller. This call is received via a high intensity light emitter mounted on an emergency vehicle and a detector mounted on or near the traffic signal.

Between January 1, 1995, and September 24, 1995, IDOT's contractor responded to 12 maintenance calls about the highway signal systems at US 14 and Lincoln Avenue and Algonquin Road. These calls involved complaints about synchronization of US 14 and the railroad crossing warning devices, flashing red lights, and no northbound green indication for Algonquin Road when railroad gates were down. The contractor investigated all of these complaints and made necessary repairs. Each time the highway traffic signal timing sequence was found to be operating as programmed.

On September 18, 1995, after the pickup truck/train collision took place at the crossing, the UP's lead signal maintainer and the IDOT contractor responded to the Fox River Grove police chief's suggestion that there might have been problems with the interaction of the railroad and highway signal systems. The police chief called the UP and IDOT, and the railroad preemption sequence was tested and the timing sequences of both the railroad and highway signal systems were found to be operating as programmed.

On September 19, 22, and 23, 1995, IDOT's contractor responded to complaints at US 14 and Lincoln Avenue and Algonquin Road and replaced equipment to correct signal system problems. On October 11, 1995, the UP reset the thumbwheel from 30 to 25 seconds (to ensure consistency throughout the railroad's property) during maintenance work on the wayside signals. UP personnel stated that IDOT was not notified of the thumbwheel setting change.

On October 24, 1995, the day before the accident, the IDOT contractor received another maintenance call that traffic was not clearing the track area properly at the Lincoln Avenue grade crossing. While inspecting the traffic signal system, he asked a railroad employee to test the circuit between the railroad signal system and the highway signal system to check the operation of the traffic signals at Lincoln Avenue. Again, he found that the railroad preemption sequence operated as programmed, with the same 18-second sequence.

At 6:40 a.m. on the day of the accident, the IDOT contractor arrived to monitor the signal system from the master controller at the US 14/Lincoln Avenue intersection. The IDOT contractor stated that he returned to monitor the system during peak traffic hours. The alarm on the master controller event log indicated that he opened the master controller at 6:52 a.m. He was not aware that, at the same time, the Fox River Grove police chief and an IDOT engineer were at the US 14/Algonquin Road intersection monitoring the signal system from a laptop computer via a modem. Just before the accident, an eastbound and a westbound train had proceeded through the Algonquin Road crossing and the police chief and IDOT engineer reported that the traffic lights were operating properly and that they visually saw traffic on Algonquin Road clear the railroad tracks before the trains arrived at the crossing. The eastbound train, however, had stopped at the station before proceeding across Algonquin Road. The next eastbound train was the accident train, an express train that did not stop at the station.

At the Safety Board's public hearing in January 1996, the UP presented construction prints dated July 14, 1995, that indicated that the railroad/highway grade crossing had a minimum of 20 seconds of warning time. IDOT representatives indicated that they had never seen these construction prints before the public hearing. The IDOT contractor testified that he used a timing sheet obtained from IDOT to check the program operation during the complaint calls. Further, IDOT representatives testified that they compared the information from this timing sheet with other documents and they believed they had a warning time of 25 to 30 seconds from the railroad signal system. The UP representatives testified that the UP designed and maintained the railroad signal system to

always provide a minimum of 20 seconds of warning time.

Tests and Research

School Bus Brake Lamps.—The rear brake lamps were tested at the Safety Board's laboratory and the lower left lamp bulb filament was stretched, which is consistent with brakes being on at the time of collision.

Event Recorder.—The trailing locomotive was equipped with a Bach-Simpson Train Monitoring and Control System Model 500 Event Recorder. The on-scene event recorder readout by the UP indicates that the throttle was moved from its maximum position "8" to "idle" at a calculated distance between 965 and 1,066 feet west of the crossing. About 2 seconds later, a full-service brake application was made at a calculated distance between 762 and 864 feet west of the crossing. The speed of the train during the throttle change and the full-service brake application was about 69 mph. About 2 seconds later, an emergency brake application was made at a calculated distance between 661 and 762 feet west of the crossing, when the train was traveling about 67 mph. Impact with the school bus occurred about 5 seconds later, when the train was traveling about 60 mph. The distance the train traveled from point of impact to the cab control car's final rest position was 1,422 feet. The Safety Board conducted its train stopping distance tests using this information.

The train's event recorder was also examined and read out by the Safety Board's Vehicle Performance Division in Washington, D.C. Laboratory personnel calculated that the throttle was moved from its maximum position "8" to "idle" between 965 and 1,066 feet west of the crossing. About 2 seconds later, the brake pipe pressure began to decrease at a calculated distance between 762 and 864 feet west of the crossing. About 2 seconds after the initial reduction in brake pipe pressure, a rapid decrease (from 77 to 11 pounds per square inch) occurred at a speed of 69 mph, and at a calculated distance between 560 and 661 feet west of the crossing. This rapid decrease in the brake pipe pressure is consistent with an emergency brake application. Impact with the school bus occurred about 6 seconds later, when the train was traveling about 60 mph. The distance the train traveled from point of impact to the cab control car's final rest position was 1,422 feet.

Recorder Circuit Board.—Although not required, the railroad uses a recorder circuit board (RCB), which is located in the railroad bungalow, to record 222 train movements within an approach circuit. The RCB records the train speeds and time provided by the railroad signal system. Once the railroad microprocessor begins sending the signal, the RCB begins recording information, including the following data elements: the average speed of the train calculated over 4 seconds after the signal is sent; the average speed of the train between the time that the signal is activated until the train reaches the island circuit (which is about 50 feet from the center of the crossing); the speed of the train 1 second before it arrives at the island circuit; and the elapsed time between the signal's activation until the train reaches the island circuit. On the day of the accident, the RCB for the accident area was malfunctioning and did not record this information. The RCB was replaced for postaccident tests conducted by the Safety Board and the data showed that the replicated accident train had 22 seconds of warning time.

Train Stopping Distance.—Safety Board investigators performed stopping distance tests using the on-scene initial event recorder data to replicate the events that occurred, such as the position change of the throttle and the full-service and emergency brake applications. The tests were conducted with the accident train traveling 70 mph (the maximum authorized track speed). The test that most closely replicated the accident had the train positioned 1,163 feet (which includes 200 feet of reaction time) west of the crossing when the test train engineer placed the throttle into idle position. About 761 feet west of the crossing, the test engineer made

a full-service brake application. About 459 feet west of the crossing, the test engineer placed the train into emergency braking. The test train stopped 1,489 feet after point of impact, which coincides with the on-scene measurement of 1,422 feet, the distance that the accident train traveled before coming to a stop after striking the school bus.

Warning Time Tests.—On October 25-26, 1995, Safety Board investigators timed approximately 15 trains to determine the amount of time that passed between when the crossing warning devices were activated and when the train arrived at the crossing. The shortest warning time was about 20 seconds and the longest warning time was 155 seconds. On the day following the accident, train 624 (the same train as the accident train) was traveling at a speed of 69-70 mph and the shortest time measured with a stopwatch was about 26 seconds before the train entered the crossing.

On October 29, 1995, Safety Board investigators conducted tests to replicate the accident train's movements and recorded warning times of 20.73 and 21.12 seconds.

In November 1995, IDOT independently conducted postaccident testing of the warning time and videotaped train traffic (both local and express) and the traffic signal. The test results indicate a 22.7-second average warning time for 70-mph eastbound trains, with a 21-second warning time for some of these trains. The warning times for the 70-mph westbound trains averaged 26.8 seconds. The results also indicate that in 34 out of 66 tests, the traffic lights provided 10 seconds or less for traffic on Algonquin Road to clear the railroad tracks.

Activation of Crossing Warning Devices Tests.—At the request of the Safety Board, Safety Engineering Associates[28] performed six tests to determine the amount of delay time

---

[28] An engineering consultant firm retained by the UP.

between the circuit activation and the actual activation of the lights and bell. The light circuits and the bell circuits were tested separately. The light circuit tests ranged from 803 to 819 milliseconds. The bell circuit tests ranged from 800 to 802 milliseconds. The average delay time for all six tests was 805 milliseconds, or 8/10 of a second.

Audibility Tests.—The Safety Board requested that the FRA conduct sound level measurements on the cab control car horn. Test results indicate that the sound level exceeded the minimum requirements of 96 decibels at a position 100 feet forward of the horn. (49 *CFR* 229.129.)

For at least 5 years, school bus manufacturers have been producing school bus bodies with sound attenuation panels to lower the noise levels on diesel-powered school buses. The bus design originally included two overhead attenuation panels. School districts subsequently began ordering entire buses with sound attenuation panels to reduce interior noise levels on buses.

Am Tran, the school bus body manufacturer, performed tests in 1990 and 1994 to compare interior engine noise levels with various materials to determine the attenuation of noise within the school bus bodies. The results indicated that the engine noise level was reduced at the driver's position by 2 decibels, and the noise level was reduced by 2 to 5 decibels for the school bus passenger positions. Preaccident tests indicated that the interior perforated ceiling panels provided sound attenuation that lowered the bus interior noise levels by reducing the reflected noise, much the way that acoustic tile lowers reflected noise in buildings.

Tests performed by Am Tran after the accident were conducted on buses similar to the accident bus, equipped with and without perforated interior overhead panels. In these tests, two noise sources were used, a bus air horn for exterior-generated noise and a bus back-up alarm for interior-generated noise. These noise sources did not match the noise levels at the

time of the accident and were chosen for demonstration purposes only.

Measurements were taken approximately 6 inches from the driver's ear. With the interior noise source placed by the rear emergency door, it produced a sound level of 78 decibels in a bus with sound attenuation materials, and 101.5 in a bus without sound attenuation materials. The noise source was then placed 50 feet from the vehicle and the exterior test produced a sound level of 78.2 decibels without sound attenuation materials and 73.5 decibels with sound attenuation materials.

The Safety Board also measured the sound[29] on a similar school bus under various circumstances. In tests conducted with traffic passing, the empty bus running (its doors closed), and the bus's radio turned on to the level it was at the time of the accident, the noise level at the driver's seat ranged from 75 to 78 decibels.

Tests were also conducted of the sound levels at the driver's position when the horn from the cab control car was sounded at distances ranging from approximately 2,500 feet away to the impact point. In those tests, the train was about 100 feet from impact before the horn sound exceeded the ambient noise levels in the bus at the driver's position. Additional tests conducted on the sound of the crossing gate bell determined that it was inaudible to a person inside the bus in the driver's position.

Sight Distance.—Safety Board investigators determined sight distances from both an eastbound train and a northbound school bus. When the bus was positioned 5 feet south of the south crossing gate, both the test train engineer and the test school busdriver had clear views of each other's vehicles for at least 2,000 feet. The test school busdriver, looking over her left shoulder, had a clear view of the train for 460

---

[29] Using a Bruel & Kjaer audiometer (Precision Sound Level Meter) type 2232, serial #1129961, calibrated with a Sound Level Calibrator type 4230, with a tone of 93.8 decibels. The audiometer reading was 94.1 decibels.

feet when the school bus was positioned in the approximate accident location.

Master Controller Event Log.—The master controller event log, which records activity at all three intersections within 1-minute intervals, indicates that the alarm went on when the IDOT contractor opened the master controller box. It also recorded the times that the preemption sequences were initiated for the two trains that preceded the accident train (as witnessed by the police chief and the IDOT engineer). The log recorded a 7:10 a.m. preemption (an eastbound train) and reported the system back on-line at 7:11 a.m. At 7:12 a.m., the log recorded a preempt sequence initiating, the alarm going off (the contractor closing the master controller box), and the conflict monitor unit flashing, which IDOT representatives believe may have been an electrical surge or short circuit caused when the traffic signal stanchion was struck by the school bus during the accident sequence. The cause of the initiation of the 7:12 a.m. preempt sequence is unknown.

Federal and State Oversight

Federal Railroad Administration.—The FRA was created in 1966 and given the responsibility by Congress to ensure public safety over the Nation's freight, passenger, and commuter rail systems. The FRA is responsible for ensuring compliance with and enforcement of all Federal rail safety regulations and has the authority to monitor the inspection of rail operations, trains, and properties. Another FRA responsibility is to compile and maintain an accident data base to determine trends and future safety concerns. Postaccident inspections by the FRA on the railroad involved in this accident revealed no defects with the railroad equipment or violations by its personnel.

One of the FRA's responsibilities is to maintain a listing of all railroad/highway grade crossings in the U.S. DOT/AAR National Highway-Rail Crossing Inventory. The information is supplied voluntarily to the Federal Government by the States and the railroads. At present, the

U.S. DOT-AAR Crossing Inventory Form (FRA 6180.71) does not have an item that captures railroad preemption/interconnection information. The instructions explain that highway traffic signals refer only to train-activated red-yellow-green signals that control street traffic over the crossing. Those persons filling out the forms are told not to count highway signals controlling nearby intersections even if they are interconnected with the crossing devices. This form is voluntary and the information previously supplied for the Algonquin Road crossing was out-of-date. The Rail-Highway Rail Crossing Accident/Incident Report (FRA 6180.57) requires railroads to indicate whether the crossing warning interconnection with highway signals was present.

Federal Highway Administration.—The FHWA is the Federal agency responsible for administering the Federal-aid Highway Program. The FHWA is responsible for reviewing, approving, and monitoring projects and providing technical assistance to the State and local transportation agencies. It also administers a national motor carrier program, with a primary mission of reducing commercial motor vehicle accidents.

National Highway Traffic Safety Administration.—The National Highway Traffic Safety Administration (NHTSA), established by the Highway Safety Act of 1970, is responsible for reducing deaths, injuries, and economic losses resulting from motor vehicle crashes. NHTSA sets and enforces safety performance standards for vehicle equipment and, through grants to State and local governments, helps them to conduct effective local highway safety programs.

Illinois Commerce Commission.—IDOT provides funding for railroad/highway grade crossing improvements under Illinois law, but the Illinois Commerce Commission has regulatory authority over railroad/highway grade crossings. The Commission's regulations have jurisdiction over both "the interested rail carrier" and the public bodies and highway authorities having jurisdiction over involved roadways, including IDOT. The State of Illinois Administration Code, Chapter III, Section 1535.350, states:

It is frequently desirable that controls for crossing signals be interconnected with those for traffic control signals at nearby highway intersections to permit highway traffic to move into the clear in advance of train movements and to permit traffic on the paralleling highway to flow while train movements are made. Where such interconnection is to be made, approval of plans shall first be received from the Illinois Commerce Commission.

Section 1535.400(d) of the Code states:

Where a rail carrier plans a major change or a reduction in marking or warning devices at any such grade crossing and no order has been issued by the Commission approving such change or reduction, the rail carrier shall give written notice of such change or reduction to the highway authority having jurisdiction over the roadway involved....

Section 1535 (e) of the Code states:

When any city, town, village, township, county or the Department proposes any highway change, including changes in highway traffic direction, which would necessitate a change in the marking, warning devices at, or construction of any crossing, notice of such proposed change shall be submitted to the rail carrier involved at least three months in advance of the date upon which the change is to be made. Copy of said notice shall be furnished to this Commission.

Joint Training.—The Safety Board reviewed training programs from the National Highway Institute, other Federal sources, and private sources. The Board found no training courses or

programs that specifically addressed the interaction and operation of railroad and highway signal systems at interconnected/preemptive railroad/highway grade crossings.

School Transportation Standards

National.—In 1992, the NHTSA published its revised *Highway Safety Program No. 17, Pupil Transportation Safety,* which provides the States guidelines for establishing pupil transportation operations. The guidelines regarding route planning, driver training, driver evaluations, etc., are general and do not give specific information. For example, the guidelines state that States should conduct careful planning and annually review school bus routes to identify safety hazards.

State.—Effective July 1, 1995, the school busdriver permitting authority in the State of Illinois was transferred from the Illinois State Board of Education (BOE) to the Illinois Secretary of State's office. However, the Illinois State BOE continues to update the school busdriver curriculum and provide school busdriver instructors with initial and refresher training.

The 1995 edition of the Illinois School Bus Driver Training curriculum states that the primary responsibility of the school busdriver is to provide safe transportation for students and calls the role of school busdriver "a very important position." In the section on "The Driver" it states that "Positioning a school bus vehicle in relationship to another object can give you a whole new perspective on your ability to judge distance in any direction." In the section on "School Bus Operations," it states:

Always keep in mind the size of your vehicle. Your vehicle is much higher than any automobile and also weighs much more. A school bus generally is twice as long and much wider than any full-sized automobile. Allow for oversize and limited maneuverability of your bus when turning.... Whether making a right or left turn, be aware that in many situations part of the REAR of your bus may project outward as you are making the turn.

The section "Trains Always Have the Right of Way" addresses railroad/highway grade crossings, stating:

> Many train/vehicle collisions could be avoided by following a few very easy but extremely important procedures when approaching a railroad crossing... require silence when approaching a crossing...all radios, tape players, etc., must be turned off or down; turn off all heaters and fans, if necessary, to hear adequately.

> Scan the surroundings for information that may indicate danger...never drive onto a railroad track until you are certain there is adequate room ahead for your ENTIRE vehicle to clear the tracks completely. It can be life threatening to begin to cross a set of railroad tracks only to find that you must stop your vehicle for traffic before you have completely cleared the tracks.

The local or State BOE has no guidance pertaining to school busdriver evaluations. An Illinois State BOE representative testified at the Safety Board's public hearing in January 1996 that Illinois does not provide any guidance other than what the law requires, and that routing is the responsibility of the local school districts because all districts are different.

Association.—The National Association of State Directors of Pupil Transportation Services (NASDPTS) is comprised of State Directors from 34 States and other school bus transportation representatives at various levels within the other States. In addition, school bus and parts manufacturers, contractors, training companies, etc., belong to the NASDPTS. The purpose of the association is to develop guidelines and standards to further the goal of safe

pupil transportation. The NASDPTS' National Standards for School Transportation provide standards for school buses and school bus operation. These guidelines address school bus routing, driver training and evaluation, and railroad/highway grade crossings. Appendix E contains information from the National Standards entitled "Recommended Procedures for School Busdrivers at Railroad/Highway Grade Crossings." The following are excerpts:

> For improved hearing, all noisy equipment (fans, etc.) should be off until the bus has cleared the crossing.

> When any school bus must stop to cross any railroad track, all passengers must be silent until the crossing is completed. A signal for silence shall be given by the driver in whatever manner is deemed suitable.

The 1995 National Standards for School Transportation recommends that:

> Every school bus shall be constructed so that the noise level taken at the ear of the occupant nearest to the primary noise source shall not exceed 85 decibels....

Action Taken After the Accident

Federal and State.—During the on-scene investigation, the Safety Board called upon the Federal oversight agencies, the FRA and the FHWA, and all the States (including the District of Columbia) to check the coordination of railroad and highway signals to ensure that vehicles have sufficient time to clear the railroad tracks. The Safety Board issued three Class 1, Urgent Safety Recommendations: H-95-15, H-95-16, and R-95-45. Safety Recommendation H-95-15 asked that State Directors of Transportation:

> Identify all railroad/highway grade crossings where control of a highway traffic signal is preempted by train movements. In cooperation with the

Federal Highway Administration and the Federal Railroad Administration, determine if the preemption allows sufficient time for vehicles to safely clear the crossing. For those crossings determined to have insufficient time for vehicles to safely clear, take immediate corrective action.

Table 3 (see pages 36-37) illustrates by State the number of preemptive/interconnected crossings reviewed as compared to each State's total number of crossings.

Safety Recommendation H-95-16 asked the FHWA to cooperate with the State Directors of Transportation and the FRA to:

Determine, at those railroad/highway grade crossings where control of a highway traffic signal is preempted by train movements, if the preemption allows sufficient time for vehicles to safely clear the crossing. For those crossings determined to have insufficient time for vehicles to safely clear, take immediate corrective action.

In a letter dated March 19, 1996, the FHWA indicated that immediately following receipt of Safety Recommendation H-95-16, the FHWA's Executive Director issued a November 2, 1995, directive to Regional and Division Administrators urging that they work closely with the States and FRA regional officials in their efforts to comply with Safety Recommendation H-95-15 to the States.

Safety Recommendation R-95-45 asked that the FRA:

Cooperate with the State Directors of Transportation and the Federal Highway Administration to determine, at those railroad/highway grade crossings where control of a highway traffic signal is preempted by train movements, if the preemption allows sufficient time for vehicles to safely clear the crossing. For those crossings determined to have

insufficient time for vehicles to safely clear, take immediate corrective action.

In a letter dated November 30, 1995, the FRA indicated that it had requested the railroads to start necessary processes to determine how many and which of their crossings should be reviewed. The FRA also indicated that it was prepared to enter information regarding crossings with preemption circuitry into the U.S. DOT/AAR National Highway-Rail Crossing Inventory. In a letter dated April 16, 1996, the Safety Board acknowledged the FRA's pledge to cooperate and assist in any way to identify and test these crossings.

The following are examples of actions taken by several States in response to the Safety Board's urgent recommendations.

The State of Virginia used a preemption technique that does not interconnect with the rail automatic warning system. This is accomplished by installing a loop on the approach between the tracks and the traffic signal. This system would have a time delay feature, thus permitting traffic signals to preempt before a vehicle can be entrapped. In a letter dated June 29, 1996, the Virginia Department of Transportation stated that its list of preempted crossings had been forwarded to the Virginia Department of Education for distribution to school busdrivers throughout the State. The list not only identifies crossing locations but also includes information to provide a better understanding of each interconnect crossing.

The Missouri Department of Transportation has developed a warning notice that will be put inside each signal house (both the road authority's and the railroad's) at each interconnected crossing location in Missouri. The Missouri Department of Transportation will print these blank forms and then type or write in the specific information pertaining to the railroad, road authority, and DOT number. This form will be placed on the wall inside the controller box.

Table 3 - Total Number of Preemptive/Interconnected Crossings Reviewed (States)

State	Total Number of Highway/Rail Grade Crossings (Public and Private)*	Total Number of Preemptive/Interconnected Crossings Reviewed	Remarks
Alabama	6,826	57	Forwarded list to the Alabama DOE
Alaska	365	6	---
Arizona	1,914	97	---
Arkansas	5,239	23	3 crossings in Morrilton upgraded
California	14,816	122	---
Colorado	3,894	25	---
Connecticut	1,274	100	School bus drivers helped to identify crossings
Delaware	532	5	---
District of Columbia	129	2	May 28, 1996, accident at Suitland Parkway crossing
Florida	5,901	276	---
Georgia	9,839	77	---
Hawaii	6	2	Both near airport
Idaho	3,163	23	Forwarded list to Idaho DOE
Illinois	19,415	243	24 crossings were adjusted
Indiana	10,777	135	---
Iowa	10,496	45	---
Kansas	12,793	46	---
Kentucky	6,675	29	---
Louisiana	7,475	29	---
Maine	2,051	22	---
Maryland	1,992	30	Includes 12 light rail crossings. List forwarded to Maryland DOE
Massachusetts	3,116	31	---
Michigan	9,398	113	---
Minnesota	9,255	91	25 crossings needed minor adjustment
Mississippi	5,483	23	---

State	Total Number of Highway/Rail Grade Crossings (Public and Private)*	Total Number of Preemptive/Interconnected Crossings Reviewed	Remarks
Missouri	9,387	24	Developed warning label
Montana	3,941	12	---
Nebraska	7,274	17	---
Nevada	660	8	---
New Hampshire	1,051	21	---
New Jersey	3,900	150	---
New Mexico	1,607	19	---
New York	9,395	78	---
North Carolina	9,386	240	---
North Dakota	7,016	13	---
Ohio	13,108	64	---
Oklahoma	6,932	56	Developed training video
Oregon	5,900	92	---
Pennsylvania	13,032	106	---
Rhode Island	356	53	---
South Carolina	4,977	92	---
South Dakota	3,692	6	---
Tennessee	6,369	72	--
Texas	21,106	330	---
Utah	1,972	2	---
Vermont	1,408	4	---
Virginia	6,595	56	Transferred list to Virginia DOE
Washington	7,137	125	---
West Virginia	5,248	10	---
Wisconsin	8,861	68	---
Wyoming	1,705	10	Developed new W10-3 sign.

* Source: *FRA Highway-Rail Crossing Accident/Incident and Inventory Bulletin (1994)*.

In response to Safety Recommendation H-95-15, the Idaho Department of Transportation conducted a review of all railroad crossings in the State of Idaho to find those with configurations similar to the accident crossing in Illinois. The Idaho Department of Transportation identified 23 crossings and conducted on-site reviews at each. The final report documenting the Idaho Department of Transportation's reviews and actions was submitted to the Safety Board on April 23, 1996. In a letter dated May 8, 1996, to the Idaho Pupil Transportation Coordinator, the Idaho State Traffic Engineer submitted this same report to the Idaho Department of Education (DOE). His letter stated:

> We believe that the information contained in the report would be of interest to all school busdrivers, and of particular interest to those drivers whose routes cross the 23 crossings in the report. Please forward this information to the appropriate school districts.

Through the Idaho DOE's *Pupil Transportation Communicator* magazine dated May 1996, every transportation supervisor in Idaho received a copy of the Idaho Department of Transportation's final report to the Safety Board. Supervisors were urged to use the report in school busdriver training.

In a letter dated May 31, 1996, to the Alabama Department of Education, the Alabama Department of Transportation forwarded its list of preempted crossings for distribution to school busdrivers throughout the State.

The Wyoming Department of Transportation developed a modified MUTCD advance warning sign (W10-3) that shows the distance in feet between the highway and the nearest rail.

The Oklahoma Department of Transportation, in conjunction with Oklahoma Operation Lifesaver, has developed a school busdriver training video. This video was the result of a mock crash conducted by the Oklahoma Department of Transportation in May 1996 between a school bus and a freight train at a crossing with configurations similar to the Algonquin Road crossing in Illinois.

Nationwide, the States found that most of the 3,360 preempted signals (more than 98 percent) were programmed with sufficient time to clear the tracks. They reported that timing had been corrected in the 52 cases in which deficiencies were found. Many of the adjustments involved reducing the pedestrian clearance time and increasing the track clearance time. Some of the States reported that pedestrian clearance times will be a continuing problem since this phase must be completed before the track clearance time.

Many of the States reported that it was beneficial and important to have the railroad representative attend the inspections so that both the highway and the railroad representatives could learn how their preemption systems worked together. The detailed responses to the Safety Board's urgent recommendations are contained in the public docket.

Task Force.—After the accident, the Secretary of the U.S. DOT convened a railroad/highway grade crossing task force to review the decisionmaking process for designing, constructing, and operating rail crossings, and to report back to him by March 1, 1996. The task force, led by the Associate Deputy Transportation Secretary, included representatives from the FRA, the FHWA, the NHTSA, the Federal Transit Administration, and the Safety Board. The task force consulted with State and local transportation authorities and conducted three public hearings to identify how railroad/highway grade crossing safety could be improved. The task force focused on the following five issue areas:

- Interconnected highway traffic signal and highway-rail crossing warning devices;

- Space available for motor vehicles between highway-rail crossings and adjacent highway-highway intersections;

- High-profile crossings and low-clearance vehicles;

- Light rail transit crossings;

- Special vehicle operating permits and information.

The report recommends actions addressing both physical and procedural deficiencies, some of which are shown in appendix F.

A longterm recommendation of the task force asked that the FHWA:

...convene a technical working group of representatives of rail crossing safety organizations to review existing standards and guidelines. One of the outputs of this group could be recommended additions and/or changes to the MUTCD, the Railroad/Highway Grade Crossing Handbook, or other appropriate documents.

The FHWA and the FRA have set up a Technical Working Group on Rail-Highway Intersections, and the FHWA has contracted with the Institute of Transportation Engineers (ITE) to facilitate the working group. Meetings were held in July and September 1996, and another is planned in January 1997.

The ITE has revised its 1979 Recommended Practice *Preemption of Traffic Signals at or Near Active Warning Railroad Grade Crossings*. The September 1996 version has included more definitive guidelines regarding the design and operation of traffic signals adjacent to railroad grade crossings with active warning devices. The document states that the intention is to supplement the requirements set forth in the MUTCD, the *Traffic Control Devices Handbook*, and the *Railroad-Highway Grade Crossing Handbook*. The document concludes with the following recommendations:

1. Develop a cooperative design process and an operating procedure that includes notifying other parties

of anticipated or proposed traffic or geometric changes, [and] maintain continuous, joint reviews among participating parties to ensure satisfactory operation to account for changing traffic conditions.

2. The distance separating the tracks from the signal must be carefully evaluated, and traffic and geometric conditions must be diligently reviewed and analyzed.

3. Complete preemption sequence time must be thoroughly analyzed, and control equipment for both the highway and railroad must be properly utilized.

Also, a National Cooperative Highway Research Program (NCHRP)[30] panel is creating a compendium of current practices entitled "NCHRP 28-12 Traffic Signal Operations Near Highway Rail Intersections," scheduled to be completed within the next year.

IDOT and the Illinois Commerce Commission—On January 15, 1996, IDOT and the Commission published a Report to the Illinois House of Representatives' Counties and Township Committee. The report identified ways to further improve the safety of school buses and rail crossings. The first action taken by IDOT was to close both the Algonquin Road and the Lincoln Avenue crossings. The State updated its crossing inventory and identified its interconnected traffic signals to ensure that these systems provided sufficient warning time.

IDOT then petitioned the Illinois Commerce Commission to provide additional warning time

---

[30] The NCHRP is administered by the Transportation Research Board, sponsored by participating members of the American Association of State Highway and Transportation Officials in cooperation with the FHWA, and is funded by participating State highway and transportation agencies.

for signal operations at the Algonquin and Lincoln crossings. The Commission staff subsequently directed, without benefit of a formal order, the UP to change the thumbwheel setting to 45 seconds. The manufacturer of the microprocessor recommended that the approach distance setting be increased to 3,840 feet. The Commission ordered the UP to extend the approach circuit to 3,594 feet. Several other changes were made by IDOT and the Fox River Grove village, including:

- Inserting a stop line on the south side of the crossing;

- Installing post-mounted traffic signals next to the stop line;

- Installing traffic signals on the railroad's south side cantilever;

- Removing post-mounted traffic signals on the north side of railroad tracks;

- Reprogramming the traffic signals on the south side to turn red before the traffic lights located on the north side of US 14;

- Eliminating the 12-second pedestrian clearance time during railroad preemption;

- Replacing the master highway traffic signal controller with another one;

- Posting a "Do Not Stop on Tracks" sign on the northbound approach to the crossing;

- Posting a "Stop Here on Red" sign with an arrow at the south side stop line;

- Posting a "Caution Walk Time Shortened When Train Approaches" sign at the pedestrian crosswalks;

- Increasing the vehicle clear-out time for Algonquin Road vehicles from 12 to 17 seconds.

In addition, the TJA School District now requires that school busdrivers stop before the railroad tracks and wait through the entire sequence unless they are the first vehicle and the light is green. After the accident, the school district provided busdrivers with copies of revised routes with hazards noted. The note concerning the accident route reads:

Notice to all TJA Personnel

Lincoln Avenue and Algonquin Road railroad crossings in the Village of Fox River Grove:

Effective immediately and until further notice, *any* TJA School Bus, whether empty or loaded, when proceeding Northbound on either of the stated thoroughfares at the railroad crossings, shall, in addition to normal State of Illinois mandated railroad crossing procedures for School Buses, NEVER attempt to cross the railroad tracks in their School Bus unless:

1. The School Bus is the first vehicle in line at the "Stop Bar" painted on the pavement South of the railroad tracks. (Stop Here on Red)

2. The School Bus driver has **already** performed the State of Illinois railroad crossing procedures.

NOTE: If the traffic light is already green after #1 and #2 above, then the School Bus driver shall *wait* through the traffic light cycle until receiving another **full green light** before proceeding. Then proceed *only* if it is safe to do so.

A survey commissioned by the Village of Fox River Grove in May 1996 revealed that only four pedestrians used the Algonquin crosswalk in a weekday 12-hour period between the daylight hours of 6 a.m. and 6 p.m.

School Bus Transportation Safety

Nationwide. — Approximately 410,000 school buses transport 23.9 million students over 4.0 billion miles across the United States annually. The NHTSA's statistics indicate that between 1984 and 1994, a total of 70 crashes occurred in which at least 1 occupant of a school bus died. Three of the 70 crashes were railroad/highway grade crossing accidents involving school buses.

Illinois. — In the State of Illinois, 21,428 school buses transport 1 million students over 225 million miles annually. TJA School District 47/155 used 72 school buses to transport about 7,500 students over 1.3 million miles during the 1994-1995 school year. Between 1984 and 1994, two accidents in Illinois involving a school bus and a train were reported. One accident resulted in an injury and the other resulted only in property damage.

Railroad/Highway Grade Crossing Safety

The FRA reports that as of 1994, about 17.5 percent of all public railroad/highway grade crossings were equipped with automatic gates, 29,325 with flashing light signals and 6,459 with other active devices.[31] The FRA also reports that between 1989 and 1994, fatalities at railroad/highway grade crossings were reduced from 725 to 542, and injuries decreased from 2,791 to 1,885. However, over 47 percent of all railroad/highway grade crossing accidents involving motor vehicles in 1994 occurred at public railroad/highway grade crossings with active warning devices.

Between 1976 and 1995, the Safety Board investigated more than 325 railroad/highway grade crossing accidents and issued more than 200 safety recommendations. Table 4 lists those

---

[31] U.S. Department of Transportation, Federal Railroad Administration, "The Highway-Rail Crossing Accident/ Incident and Inventory Bulletin," No. 17, CY 1994, published July 1995.

Table 4 — Safety Board Investigations of Grade Crossing Accidents Involving School Buses

Date	Place	Number of deaths/injured
10/02/1967	Waterloo, Nebraska	4 fatal, 9 injured
3/24/1972	Congers, New York	5 fatal, 44 injured
10/23/1974	Aragon, Georgia	7 fatal, 71 injured
8/08/1976	Stratton, Nebraska	9 fatal, 8 injured
4/12/1984	Carrsville, Virginia	1 fatal, 26 injured
9/27/1984	Port St. Lucie, Florida	2 fatal, 1 injured

crossing accidents involving school buses that the Safety Board investigated.

All of these accidents occurred at passive crossings (no bell, lights, or gates) except for those in Stratton, Nebraska, and Port St. Lucie, Florida. The Safety Board has, over the past 30 years, issued school bus safety recommendations regarding:

- School bus routing to avoid railroad/highway grade crossings;

- Methods of looking for trains at crossings;

- School authorities monitoring drivers at railroad/highway grade crossings;

- Conspicuity and audibility of train's lights and horns.

Operation Lifesaver

Operation Lifesaver, Inc., (OL) is an active, continuous public information and education program designed to help prevent and reduce railroad/highway grade crossing accidents. The UP founded OL in Idaho in 1972. Today, OL is sponsored cooperatively by Federal, State, and local government agencies, highway safety organizations, and the Nation's railroads. In fiscal year 1995, the national OL program received $300,000 from the FHWA in general support, and approximately $100,000 from the FRA in project-specific grants.

OL promotes crossing safety by coordinating speaking engagements by trained and certified presenters, responding to media inquiries, providing testimony at public hearings, and distributing educational materials. OL has a specific program designed to be presented before school busdrivers that emphasizes, among other things, the need to maintain quiet in the vicinity of railroad crossings and the importance of assuring that when a driver starts across the tracks there is adequate room on the other side. Every State, except Hawaii, has an OL program coordinator, and the Safety Board has issued safety recommendations to OL in the past.

ANALYSIS

General

The weather was clear and dry at the time of the accident and, although the sun was rising, neither the school busdriver nor the train engineer identified the sun as impairing visibility. Safety Board tests conducted about the same time of day did not indicate that the sun posed a visibility problem. The railroad track approaching the accident site is straight and provides an unobstructed view of the Algonquin Road grade crossing. A review of track inspection records revealed no anomalies, and the train engineer took no exception with the track.

A review of the maintenance records and inspections both before and after the accident revealed that neither the train locomotive nor the cab control car had any mechanical problems. The maintenance records for the 3-year-old school bus indicated no mechanical problems. The busdriver did not indicate that she had any difficulty (mechanical or otherwise) with the operation of the school bus, and the postaccident examination of the school bus did not reveal any discrepancies.

The engineer was experienced in operating the commuter passenger train over the territory and had been observing the appropriate rules and procedures, in accordance the UP operating practices, while operating the train. Also, his past efficiency and safety audits revealed compliance with the UP rules. Data from the event recorder correspond with the engineer's statement of his observations and actions before impact, and no evidence indicates that he might have been fatigued.

The school busdriver had held a valid school busdriver license for 8 years, had no record of violations or accidents, had passed all applicable tests, and had taken more than the required number of busdriver training courses, including the OL course addressing grade crossing hazards. Although a substitute bus-driver, she had had substantial school bus driving experience in the past 3 years. Witnesses said that she stopped the school bus before the crossing and that she looked and listened for oncoming trains. From her actions, it appears that she was aware of the correct procedures to follow when approaching a grade crossing, and no evidence indicates that she might have been fatigued.

Toxicological tests performed on blood and urine specimens taken from the train engineer and the school busdriver several hours after the accident were negative for alcohol and illicit drugs. The fact that the analgesic, antihistamine, and nasal decongestant were present in the busdriver's urine specimen is consistent with her statement that she had taken an over-the-counter cold medication at 9 or 10 p.m. the night before the accident. The fact that analgesic and antihistamine were found in the urine, but not in the blood, indicates that most of the medication had metabolized and should not have affected the busdriver's abilities.

Therefore, the Safety Board concludes that neither the weather, the position of the sun, the track, nor the mechanical condition of the train or of the school bus either caused or contributed to the collision. The train engineer was qualified to perform his duties and was in compliance with the hours-of-service requirements, and the busdriver was trained and experienced to drive school buses. Neither alcohol nor drug use by the train engineer or the school busdriver was a factor in the accident.

Several factors contributed to an expeditious emergency response. The Fox River Grove police chief witnessed and immediately reported the collision. Motorists equipped with cellular phones also called 911 to report the accident. Additionally, fire and rescue equipment was close by because a volunteer fire department was located 350 feet southeast of the collision site. The clear weather and the dry road enabled the emergency equipment to arrive at the scene without difficulty. As a result, critically injured school bus passengers were quickly triaged and transported to nearby trauma centers, and the other injured passengers were directly conveyed to and treated at local hospitals. Therefore, the Safety Board concludes that emergency response personnel reacted promptly to the emergency and acted effectively and efficiently at the collision site, and that the emergency response efforts were well coordinated.

Immediately following the accident, the Safety Board called upon the FRA, the FHWA, and the States, including the District of Columbia, to check the coordination of railroad and highway signals to ensure that vehicles have sufficient time to clear the railroad tracks. The Safety Board issued three Urgent Safety Recommendations: H-95-15, H-95-16, and R-95-45 to this effect. Because all the States and the District of Columbia have complied with its intent, Safety Recommendation H-95-15 is herewith classified "Closed—Acceptable Action." Further, because all the States and the District of Columbia have completed their reviews of railroad/highway grade crossings having pre-emptive signals, Safety Recommendation H-95-16 is herewith classified "Closed—Acceptable Action." For the same reason, Safety Recommendation R-95-45 is herewith classified "Closed—Acceptable Action."

The following analysis addresses the school busdriver's performance; the school district oversight, including bus routing and busdriver monitoring and evaluating procedures; the road design; the railroad/highway signal interaction; the State and railroad coordination and communication, including oversight of the signal system integration; and the injury and survival factors in the school bus.

Accident Analysis

After reviewing the train event recorder data, railroad and highway signal system design and calculations, postaccident testing, and witness statements, the Safety Board considers that the following event sequence likely occurred. Train 624 approached the railroad/highway grade crossing on a clear signal. Traveling 64 mph, it crossed the narrow band shunt, which was 3,080 feet from the crossing, 32 seconds[32] before impact. Then, 24 seconds before collision, the railroad system signaled the highway system of the approach of the train, which was 2,400 feet from the crossing and traveling 66 mph. The preemption cycle began 1 second later for the highway traffic signal system; about the same time, the train engineer first saw the school bus on the grade crossing. Still traveling 66 mph, the train was 2,300 feet from the crossing. The pedestrian phase in the highway traffic signal system ended 12 seconds before impact; the train was then traveling 69 mph and was 1,200 feet from the crossing. Ten seconds before the collision, the train engineer began sounding the horn as well as making a throttle reduction to idle and a full-service brake application; at this point, the train was still traveling 69 mph and was 1,000 feet from the crossing. The US 14 yellow indication and the intersection red indication ended 7 ½ and 6 seconds, respectively, before impact. Concurrently, the train was traveling 67 mph and was 600 feet from the crossing when a green indication would have been displayed for Algonquin Road. The engineer placed the train into emergency braking 500 feet from the collision site and 5 seconds before the collision.

The school bus had stopped on the south side of the tracks, proceeded across the tracks, and stopped at US 14 for a red signal indication. The crossing warning devices activated with the lights flashing, the bell sounding, and the gates descending. The passengers in the rear of the bus initially joked about the northern crossing gate descending and striking the school bus on its left side near the 10th window. Then, seeing the train, they yelled warnings about its

---

[32] Approximate values are used for this discussion because timing values can fluctuate within railroad and highway signal systems as designed.

approach to the busdriver. Traveling about 60 mph, the train struck the bus at a 75-degree angle in the left-side rear and penetrated as much as 3 1/3 feet into the passenger area. The bolts that secured the bus body and chassis sheared; the body and chassis separated. The bus body rotated counterclockwise, scraped the ground, struck and knocked down a traffic light signal support, and came to rest about 195 degrees from its original orientation. The chassis rotated counterclockwise, struck the side of the train, and came to rest in the road about 45 degrees from its original orientation.

The Safety Board considers that the highway traffic signal sequence may have taken 21 seconds and would only apply when the light for US 14 displayed a green indication within 3 seconds of the preempt signal. However, the school busdriver indicated that the traffic signal displayed a red indication as she approached the crossing and proceeded slowly across the railroad tracks. The traffic signal for northbound Algonquin Road displayed a red indication for 3 seconds or more; therefore, US 14 would have had a green indication before the preempt signal. The occurrence of a 21-second traffic signal sequence at the time of the accident is unlikely. The Safety Board determined that the traffic signal had an 18-second cycle before the green indication for northbound Algonquin Road displayed and that the US 14 traffic signal displayed a red indication for several seconds before the collision. The school busdriver said that she never saw the traffic signal for Algonquin Road display a green indication; the passenger who had been assisting the busdriver reported that the busdriver's attention had been diverted to the rear of the bus before impact.

School Busdriver Performance

The school busdriver was unfamiliar with the route that included the queuing area and the traffic light sequence at the intersection of Algonquin Road and US 14. She stated that she stopped the bus on the south side of the tracks, did not see any trains or the crossing warning devices activated, and then slowly crossed the

railroad tracks. She added that the traffic light for Algonquin Road was displaying a red indication and she believed that she would need to proceed across the tracks to trip a sensor that would trigger the traffic light to display a green indication. The busdriver said that she drove over the stop line to wait for the light to change.

The distance between the crossing gate and stop line north of the tracks on Algonquin Road was about 20 feet. However, the school bus was 38 feet 4 inches long and the overhang of the train was about 3 feet on each side; therefore, at least 3 feet of the school bus was in the path of the train. The right and left side of the bus were, respectively, overlapping the tracks and in the path of the train because the bus was at a 75-degree angle to the tracks. No evidence indicates that the school busdriver ever attempted to determine whether her bus had adequate space. She stated that, "It never entered my mind that there wasn't enough room for the bus to fit," and that she did not know the rear of her bus was in the train path. The other school busdrivers who had traversed this crossing knew from their experience that the space was too short for a school bus, and they would stop on the south side of the railroad crossing.

The Safety Board investigation of a 1993 collision[33] in Fort Lauderdale, Florida, involving a gasoline tank truck and a train underscores the need that motorists understand vehicle positioning when stopped at a railroad crossing. In the Fort Lauderdale case, due to congested traffic at a work zone, the truckdriver was stopped at a railroad crossing when its gate came down and struck his truck hood. Because the gate was not parallel to the rail, the distance between the two varied and was 14 feet at its narrowest point. The truck and its hood were 22 and 6 feet long, respectively. Had the gate struck the hood windshield, the front of the

---

[33] Highway Accident Report--*Gasoline Tank Truck/Amtrak Train Collision and Fire in Fort Lauderdale, Florida, March 17, 1993* (NTSB/HAR-94/01).

truck would have been about 8 feet from the east rail. The train overhang was 3 feet on each side, which left about 5 feet of clearance between the truck and the train.

After the accident, a Safety Board investigator who was seated in a similar vehicle with its air ride seat fully extended measured the sight distance and was able to see the ground 16 feet in front of the bumper. Therefore, the truckdriver probably was not able to see the track directly in front of his truck. He may have thought that he had encroached on the railroad track and needed to move forward. He proceeded to drive across the tracks and was struck by the passenger train. A fire subsequently erupted killing the truckdriver and five motorists on the opposite side of the crossing. Had the truckdriver remained in the position under the crossing gate, he would have avoided the collision.

The Illinois school busdriver training curriculum addresses the importance of recognizing the position of the school bus in relation to other vehicles and objects. No specific or practical instruction (except the road test administered when a driver first obtains a school busdriver permit) is provided to ensure that a busdriver understands positioning on the road. The school busdriver in this accident was trained and experienced, but she did not accurately judge the position of her vehicle and acknowledged that she did not know where the rear of her bus was in relation to the railroad tracks. Other drivers familiar with this route were aware of vehicle positioning, but not as a result of training. Therefore, the Safety Board concludes that the guidance provided in the Illinois school busdriver training curriculum about vehicle positioning in relation to the roadway is ineffective. Consequently, the Safety Board believes that the State of Illinois should advise school busdrivers of the circumstances of this accident and provide the busdrivers with practical training about vehicle positioning on the road, especially at railroad/highway grade crossings.

During its investigation, the Safety Board found that no specific guidance is provided at the national level about vehicle positioning and available space at railroad/highway grade crossings. The OL is developing a training videotape that addresses school bus vehicle positioning at railroad/highway grade crossings, and this should provide valuable guidance on this subject to those school busdrivers who receive OL training. However, other school busdrivers throughout the United States who are exposed to short queuing areas near such grade crossings may not be provided with the OL information. Therefore, the Safety Board believes that the NASDPTS should advise its members of the circumstances of this accident and provide guidance about vehicle positioning on the road, especially at railroad/highway grade crossings.

According to the school busdriver and the passengers in the front of the bus, they had not seen the crossing warning devices activate or the train approaching, nor had they heard the crossing gate strike the bus. The front of the bus had likely passed the warning light pole before the lights began flashing. Once positioned forward of visual cues, the busdriver and forward passengers would have had to look rearward at an angle to have seen the danger cues, which they did not. The passengers in the rear of the bus who first saw the crossing gate strike the bus initially joked about it. However, when they saw the train coming and heard the horn blowing, they began yelling at the busdriver to move the bus. As more passengers became aware of the approaching train and began yelling, the noise level in the bus increased and caught the attention of the busdriver and passengers up front, who did not initially grasp what those yelling were attempting to convey. The busdriver looked in the rearview mirror at this time; hence, the increased sound likely had the unintended consequence of distracting her attention from the traffic signal, which displayed the green indication for 2 to 6 seconds before the collision. Because the busdriver did not realize that her bus was in the train's path, whether she would have reacted to the crossing warning devices had she seen and heard them activate is unknown. The Safety Board therefore concludes that, had the school busdriver discerned the combined visual and audible warnings that a train was approaching, she might have had sufficient time to recognize the hazard and move the bus before impact.

From the school district's experience, playing the AM/FM radio on a school bus had a pacifying effect on its passengers. One of the eight radio speakers on the bus was positioned on the left side wall next to the busdriver's head. Safety Board tests indicated that when the radio was turned on, the busdriver could not hear the train horn. Regardless of the possible passenger pacification safety benefits that may result from playing the radio on a school bus, placing a radio speaker adjacent to a busdriver's head is unnecessary to achieve this effect. Therefore, the Safety Board believes that the NASDPTS should develop guidelines for the appropriate placement of radio speakers on school buses and disseminate these guidelines to its members. The Board further believes that the NASDPTS should advise its members to check their school district buses and disable any radio speakers located immediately adjacent to school busdrivers' heads.

The Safety Board recognizes that perforated ceiling liners, as on the accident school bus, probably provide a benefit by reducing the noise level and thereby lessening the distractions for busdrivers. However, tests conducted by both the manufacturer and the Safety Board revealed that in a bus with a perforated ceiling liner, the sounds from the rear to the front of the bus were reduced as much as 25 decibels compared with a bus without the liner. The perforated ceiling liner reduced the volume of the train horn and the warnings from the bus passengers. The Safety Board is unable to determine in this accident, whether sound attenuation materials affected the busdriver's ability to discern the audible warnings. The Safety Board therefore believes that NHTSA should determine what effect school bus sound attenuation materials

have on the ability of a busdriver to discern both interior and exterior audible warnings.

School District Oversight

Although school bus routes should avoid crossing railroad tracks, a railroad grade crossing on this route could not be avoided because of the limited paths available to access the residential area that the school bus was serving. However, methods to identify railroad/highway grade crossings hazards can be employed, and the school district specified three procedures to identify hazards on its school bus routes. The school transportation director described these procedures as 1) planning and monitoring the routes and consulting a commuter train schedule for those that crossed railroad tracks, 2) driving the route in his car after a hazard had been reported, and 3) noting hazards or unusual conditions on the back of the busdrivers' route maps.

There are problems with these procedures. First, using a commuter train schedule to identify route hazards is an unreliable method because trains and buses do not always run on time, as evidenced in this accident. In addition, such schedules provide no information about freight train movements or the characteristics of trains and railroad grade crossings. Second, driving the routes can be an effective method of hazard evaluation if it is done routinely. The transportation director could cite only one occasion during his 15 years of experience in which he drove a school bus route in response to a hazard report. This information indicates that this method of hazard identification was infrequently employed by the TJA School District. Finally, no notations about hazards or unusual conditions were found on the back of the accident route map or any other route map. The busdrivers familiar with the accident route had adopted strategies to avoid remaining on the tracks at Algonquin Road and an adjacent railroad crossing. However, these practices had been neither formalized as written instructions for busdrivers nor discussed by the busdrivers familiar with the route with other school busdrivers or school officials.

Although all busdrivers should be encouraged to report perceived hazards to school authorities, the school transportation director is responsible for periodically monitoring the school bus routes and the busdrivers. The TJA transportation director stated that he monitored the school bus routes; however, he did not identify the Algonquin Road grade crossing as a hazard. The policy for drivers to share information on route hazards was not enforced and was, therefore, useless, as the regular and substitute drivers did not share their driving strategies with each other or school officials. Had a note with a special instruction about the short queuing area been provided, the accident busdriver might have stopped on the south side of the crossing to wait for a green signal indication and thus have avoided the accident. The Safety Board therefore concludes that the methods employed by the school district to identify and evaluate route hazards were ineffective. Furthermore, had the school district ensured that all school busdrivers exchanged information about any identified route hazards, such as the short queuing area, the accident busdriver might have avoided the collision.

The State of Illinois requires that school busdrivers be evaluated regularly. The school transportation director is responsible for ensuring that school busdrivers are monitored and evaluated. The monitoring of substitute school busdrivers especially should be conducted because substitute drivers may not be familiar with the different bus routes, existing hazards, or bus equipment. Although the accident busdriver frequently had substituted over the past years, her driving performance had not been monitored or evaluated. The Safety Board therefore concludes that had the regular and substitute school busdrivers been monitored during their morning routes, school officials might have been aware that the regular school busdrivers habitually stopped on the south side of the Algonquin Road grade crossing to wait for a green indication.

The Safety Board believes that the TJA School District should develop and implement a program for the identification of school bus route hazards and should routinely monitor and evaluate all regular and substitute school busdrivers. The Safety Board additionally believes that the NASDPTS should encourage its members to develop and implement a program for the identification of school bus route hazards and to routinely monitor and evaluate all regular and substitute school busdrivers. Further, the Safety Board believes that the NASDPTS should advise its members to consider railroad/highway grade crossing accident histories when establishing school bus routes.

Road Design

Illinois State law prohibits driving onto a railroad grade crossing unless the other side of the grade crossing has sufficient space to accommodate the vehicle without obstructing rail traffic. After the road widening was completed at the US 14 and Algonquin Road intersection in 1989, the distances from the northern rail and crossing gate to the stop line were 28.5 and 21 feet, respectively. The IDOT design for the road widening failed to allow for space in the queuing area sufficient to accommodate vehicles such as dump trucks, tractor-semitrailers, mobile homes, and school and commercial buses. The accident school busdriver could have known about the short queuing area through a school district route hazard identification system, had such a system been available. However, other motorists would not have had the advantage of using a school district hazard identification system, even had one been in place.

Because no road signs were posted to provide information on the available space in the queuing area, these other motorists might be unable to determine whether the queuing area could adequately accommodate their vehicles. IDOT could have posted signs indicating the length of the queuing area, prohibiting motorists with vehicles in excess of that length from crossing the tracks during a red indication, and instructing those motorists to wait on the south side of the tracks for a green indication. Another traffic signal also could have been installed to coordinate with the intersection light. IDOT has installed a stop line, traffic signs, and traffic signals on the south side of the grade crossing since the collision. Therefore, the Safety Board concludes that IDOT had not employed sufficient measures before the accident to prevent vehicles from encroaching on the railroad tracks while stopped at the north side of the grade crossing. On this basis, the Safety Board believes that IDOT should review all railroad/highway grade crossings in Illinois to ensure that vehicles have adequate space and time to clear the crossing before the arrival of a train.

This collision and the March 1993 Fort Lauderdale accident indicate that motorists often do not recognize the position of a vehicle in relation to an approaching train at a railroad/highway grade crossing. Automatic gates in the down position and stop lines offer visual references to define a train right-of-way. The MUTCD specifies the location of the railroad warning devices and the stop lines relative to the railroad tracks. However, not all grade crossings have these visual references. These accidents illustrate that motorists may not be aware that they are in the train path, even at crossings equipped with warning devices and stop lines. The Safety Board therefore believes that the FHWA should develop guidelines and amend the MUTCD to provide methods to delineate the area (zone) that a train, or its cargo, or both, may occupy on the track or tracks of a railroad grade crossing so motorists have visual reference points to ascertain whether their vehicle is encroaching on the travel path of the train, or its cargo, or both. The Safety Board also believes that the FHWA should disseminate safety information, in cooperation with NHTSA and OL, once guidelines are developed, to national, State, police, public service, and safety agencies to provide a training and education module to inform motorists of the methods developed to delineate the area (zone) that a train, or its cargo, or both, may occupy on the track or tracks of a railroad grade crossing.

Also, the Safety Board believes that NHTSA and OL should disseminate safety information, in cooperation with the FHWA, once it develops guidelines, to national, State, police, public service, and safety agencies to provide a training and education module to inform motorists of the methods developed to delineate the area (zone) that a train, or its cargo, or both, may occupy on the track or tracks of a railroad grade crossing.

Railroad/Highway Signal Interaction

All railroads are required by the FRA to provide a minimum of 20 seconds of warning time before train arrival at a grade crossing.[34] The FHWA-funded February 1991 report[35] by the University of Tennessee found that both extremely short and excessively long warning times are dangerous. Warning times in excess of 30 to 40 seconds were found to cause many motorists to engage in risky crossing behavior. Most motorists expect a train to arrive within 20 seconds of traffic control device activation.

Before October 11, 1995, at the Fox River Grove collision site, the thumbwheel setting for the preempt was set at 30 seconds; however, 2 weeks before the accident, the UP reset the thumbwheel to 25 seconds. Nonetheless, all postaccident tests conducted by the FRA, the Safety Board, the UP, and IDOT resulted in a warning time of 20 seconds or more before a train reached the crossing.

Because the highway traffic signal system at the accident site did not operate in a coordinated mode after it was installed in January 1990, northbound traffic on Algonquin Road waited only 6 seconds before receiving a green indication. Therefore, traffic would have had 14 seconds or more to clear the grade crossing before the arrival of a train traveling 69 mph, as

[34] 49 *CFR* Part 234.225.

[35] Report No. FHWA-SA-91-007, 1991.

was train 624. In October 1994, IDOT installed new traffic signal controllers that automatically displayed the 12-second pedestrian clearance phase from 5:45 a.m. to 10 p.m., and the traffic on Algonquin Road then waited a minimum of 18 seconds for a green indication. As a result, traffic would only have 2 to 6 seconds (20- to 24-second warning time, respectively) to clear the grade crossing.

After receiving complaints about the short green indication for Algonquin Road, IDOT and its representatives checked the timing sequence numerous times to ascertain whether the highway signal system was operating as programmed. Each time they found it to be so operating. The IDOT contractor had never inspected the highway signal system during a time that 70-mph commuter trains were in operation. The least time duration of a green indication for northbound Algonquin Road would result from a commuter train approaching the grade crossing. Because the contractor had only been checking the signal system against its program, he had never considered the critical element — the length of time the green indication provided for northbound Algonquin Road before the arrival of a train. Then, the day before the accident, he recognized that the time of day might have been a factor in the complaints and, as a result of this recognition, he was inspecting the highway signal system at the Lincoln Road and US 14 intersection at the time of the accident.

IDOT representatives and the signal manufacturer indicated that the contractor at the master controller could not have manipulated the highway signal system from the Lincoln Road intersection to have caused a preempt signal at the time of the accident. The IDOT engineer monitoring the highway traffic signal system on the laptop computer at Algonquin Road had the capability to initiate a preempt signal by downloading a program, changing it, and uploading it again. However, these actions would have taken several minutes to perform, and they would have been recorded on the master controller log had they occurred. Another possibility was that the preempt sequence could

have been caused by an emergency vehicle arriving on the scene of the accident. However, the first emergency vehicle responding to the scene either did not have the equipment capable of signaling a preempt sequence or did not have the equipment activated at the time. The Safety Board was unable to determine what caused the preempt sequence that occurred at 7:12 a.m. on the day of the accident.

The RCB was not recording on the day of the accident. During postaccident Safety Board tests, the RCB was replaced and it recorded data for the tests. Two tests were conducted to replicate the accident train event recorder data. Both tests provided 22 seconds of warning time. The results indicate that the maximum green time based on the recorded data could have been between 2 to 4 seconds before the train arrived at the crossing.

Railroads are not required to install nor maintain RCB equipment at railroad/highway grade crossings. This equipment is primarily designed as a diagnostic tool for railroad signal maintenance personnel. However, information recorded by RCBs or similar equipment can be used to determine the performance of the grade crossing devices. If used for this purpose, RCBs, similar railroad recording devices, and corresponding highway recording devices can significantly improve the opportunities for railroad and highway personnel to accurately determine warning times at interconnected/preemptive grade crossings. For example, had the RCB at the accident site been recording information, and had IDOT and UP maintenance personnel reviewed this information after the September, 1995 accident or when evaluating complaints of a short green signal, the IDOT contractor may have recognized the actual warning times that the railroad signal system provided. The Safety Board concludes that the installation and use of railroad and highway signal recording devices at interconnected/preemptive grade crossings can improve opportunities for highway and railroad personnel to determine if the signals are coordinated and operating properly. The Safety Board therefore believes that the U.S. Department of Transportation should require the use and maintenance of railroad and highway traffic signal recording devices on all new and improved installations at railroad/highway grade crossings that have active warning train detection systems and are interconnected/preemptive to highway signal systems. The devices should record sufficient parameters to allow railroad and highway personnel to readily determine if the highway signals and railroad-activated warning devices are coordinated and operating properly. The Safety Board also believes that the U.S. Department of Transportation should require that existing recording devices for railroad and highway signals systems at interconnected/preemptive grade crossings be retained or upgraded as necessary, and that these recording devices should be maintained and that the information from these devices be used during comprehensive and periodic joint inspections. Had the RCB at the accident site been recording information on the day of the accident, the Safety Board could have used the information during its investigation to determine the exact warning time provided by the railroad signal system for the accident train.

The school busdriver stated that she never saw a green indication; the student assisting her said that the busdriver was looking in the mirror toward the rear of the bus just before the collision. From the evidence, the green indication was displayed 2 to 6 seconds before impact. Research[36] shows that the average time for a driver to perceive and react to a traffic light change is 2.56 seconds; the Safety Board calculated that it would take 1.8 seconds for the accident schoolbus to accelerate out of the path of the approaching train. Therefore, the driver would have needed about 4.4 seconds to perceive/react and move the bus far enough forward to avoid the collision. However, be-

cause the school busdriver was distracted seconds before the impact by the passengers and had diverted her attention to the rear of the bus, the 2 to 6 seconds was not sufficient time for her to clear the tracks before the arrival of Train 624. The Safety Board concludes that the highway traffic signal hardware (heads, controllers, masts, posts, and loop detectors) conformed to design standards and operated as intended, but the signal system did not provide sufficient time for northbound traffic on Algonquin Road to clear the grade crossing. The Safety Board also concludes that the highway traffic signal system before the collision provided a green indication for northbound Algonquin Road for 2 to 4 seconds based on the postaccident testing, or for 2 to 6 seconds based on the highway signal system programming.

No national data base, including the U.S. DOT/AAR grade crossing inventory, currently identifies and documents railroad/highway grade crossings in which the railroad signal system preempts or interconnects with the highway signal system. Having this documentation available in a data base would have been valuable, especially after the Safety Board issued its urgent recommendations following this accident. The Safety Board concludes that had a data base containing grade crossing signal system information been available after this accident, the States could have more readily identified and then inspected specific crossings to ensure that the signal systems posed no hazards. Therefore, the Safety Board believes that the FRA should expand the U.S. DOT/AAR National Highway-Rail Crossing Inventory to include information on highway/railroad grade crossings having preemptive or interconnected signals, and should review and update the inventory, once modified, annually.

State and Railroad Coordination and Communication

The IDOT and the railroad had exchanged various documents before the accident that

---

[36] G. Johansson and K. Rumar, "Drivers' Brake Reaction Times," *Human Factors*, Vol. 13, No. 1 (1971), pp. 22-27; G.H. Robinson et al, "Visual Search by Automobile Drivers," *Human Factors*, Vol. 14, No. 4 (1972), pp. 315-323.

included information about the warning times of the railroad signal system. After the accident, IDOT reviewed the documents and thought that they had been given 30 and 25 seconds of warning time, respectively, before and after October 11, 1995. During the review, the most misunderstood term was "warning time." IDOT personnel had concluded from the construction prints, numerous letters and memos, and the thumbwheel setting, that a minimum warning time of either 25 or 30 seconds was provided between the time the crossing warning devices were activated and a train reached the crossing.

The warning time provided by the railroad signal system does not always equate to the thumbwheel setting (25 seconds at the time of the accident). Postaccident testing found that the warning time may have been less than 25 seconds, although never less than 20 seconds, as required. Although IDOT acknowledged that it understood the railroad terminology for "preempt" and "interconnect," it did not understand that additional time must be built into the thumbwheel setting to ensure the minimum warning time because of delay times in the circuitry. IDOT officials, according to testimony, did not understand that the railroad was only providing a 20-second minimum warning time through the thumbwheel setting.

Before the accident, State and railroad signal technicians had discussed the signal systems, and several design reviews of the accident grade crossing had also been conducted. IDOT representatives had responded to the intersection on several occasions to check for short green indications. However, until the day of the accident, they had checked the operating program of the traffic signal system and not recognized that Algonquin Road did not receive a signal in time for traffic to clear the railroad tracks. IDOT did not understand the timing. According to the IDOT engineering technician, he programmed the highway signal system conforming to his experiences of 20 to 30 seconds; he never used any written information on the warning time from the railroad. Therefore, the Safety Board concludes that IDOT had programmed its highway signal

system without applying the minimum warning time information from the railroad.

The UP had reset the thumbwheel from 30 to 25 seconds on October 11, 1995, but it did not notify IDOT of the change. The Safety Board is unable to determine whether IDOT would have reacted had they been notified. Even after the accident, IDOT thought that the 25-second thumbwheel setting meant 25 seconds of warning time. Also, IDOT had not modified the programming previously, even though the 25-second warning time was referenced before the change in the thumbwheel setting.

IDOT and its contractors had opportunities to identify the short green indication for northbound Algonquin Road during 70-mph train operations and, as a result, could have modified the highway traffic signal system or requested more time from the railroad to ensure a sufficient interval for traffic to clear the crossing. However, communication about the interconnected signal systems was not effective between the State and the railroad. The Safety Board therefore concludes that had an effective communication system existed between IDOT and the UP about the interconnected signal systems, IDOT might have understood that the railroad had provided through the thumbwheel setting only a minimum of 20 seconds of warning time before the arrival of a train at the grade crossing.

In three previous investigations, Safety Board determined that ineffective communications between highway departments and the railroads caused or contributed to grade crossing accidents. First, in the March 1993 Fort Lauderdale accident,[37] highway engineers designed a work zone that caused traffic to congest at the railroad/highway grade crossing. The Safety Board found that the highway engineers had not

---

[37] Highway Accident Report--*Collision of Amtrak Train No. 88 with Rountree Transport and Rigging, Inc., Vehicle on CSX Transportation, Inc., Railroad near Intercession City, Florida, on November 30, 1993* (NTSB/HAR-95/01).

"adequately considered either the traffic congestion or the resulting obstruction of the railroad/highway grade crossing." In the November 1993 Intercession City, Florida, accident involving a low clearance, overdimension, overweight vehicle, the Safety Board found that the Florida Department of Transportation did not ensure that the railroad had been notified of the vehicle's movement over its grade crossing. Finally, in the May 1995 collision at a grade crossing near Sycamore, South Carolina,[38] the Safety Board reported:

> Recent interviews and previous accident investigations conducted by the Safety Board have revealed that the degree of communication and cooperation between railroads and public entities regarding grade crossing activities varies widely. Railroad and public officials tend to communicate more on activities that involve funding of active crossings or the installation and maintenance of active warning devices, or that are likely to generate public complaints. The same level of communication does not exist when it comes to other crossing maintenance activities, particularly as they relate to passive crossings. CSX Transportation (CSXT), which operates more than 20,000 miles of track, performs crossing profile maintenance to ensure track vertical and horizontal alignment and adequate drainage, while State, local, and sometimes private entities are responsible for maintaining the alignment of the crossing approaches. When crossing maintenance is performed, the CSXT does not always advise respective entities of these activities. By the same token, in some cases, local entities perform work to realign crossing approaches without informing the railroads. Thus, the Safety Board concludes that railroads and

public entities do not routinely communicate with each other on grade crossing maintenance activities.

Misunderstandings about grade crossing systems can be manifested through differences in terminology, construction and maintenance designs and practices, and inspection and operation methods. The Safety Board therefore believes that the U.S. Secretary of Transportation should develop a common glossary of railroad/highway grade crossing terms and disseminate this glossary to railroads and public entities. Although many efforts have been made to address grade crossing safety, no single coordinated program has been available to ensure effective communication on all aspects of grade crossing safety between transportation modes. The Safety Board concludes that, had a coordinated program to ensure effective communication between transportation modes about all aspects of grade crossing safety been in operation, the ineffective communication between IDOT and the railroad might never have occurred. The Safety Board therefore believes that IDOT should train its personnel and contractors involved in the design, inspection, and maintenance of highway signals at highway/railroad crossings to ensure that they understand the integration and working relationship to the railroad and highway signal systems.

The Safety Board further believes that the U.S. Secretary of Transportation should develop a comprehensive and periodic railroad/highway grade crossing safety inspection program to be conducted jointly by railroads and public entities and also require that railroads and public entities coordinate changes to railroad/highway grade crossings before implementation.

Development of an inspection program for the more than 314,000 railroad/highway grade crossings will be a significant challenge. However, the U.S. DOT has successfully implemented a similar national inspection program. As a result of recommendations from the Safety Board investigation of the 1967 Silver River

---

[38] Highway Accident Report--*Highway/Rail Grade Crossing Collision near Sycamore, South Carolina, May 2, 1995* (NTSB/HAR-96/01).

Bridge collapse in Point Pleasant, West Virginia,[39] and other bridge collapses, the FHWA developed the National Bridge Inventory and inspection programs. These efforts have resulted in the inspection and safety review of over 577,000 bridges nationwide.

Also, the Safety Board believes that the U.S. Secretary of Transportation should notify, in cooperation with the American Association of State Highway and Transportation Officials, the National Association of County Engineers, the American Public Works Association, the Institute of Transportation Engineers, the AAR, the American Short Line Railroad Association, and the American Public Transit Association, railroads and public entities about the importance of exchanging information about railroad/highway grade crossings. Furthermore, the Safety Board believes that the American Association of State Highway and Transportation Officials, the National Association of County Engineers, the American Public Works Association, the Institute of Transportation Engineers the AAR, the American Short Line Railroad Association, and the American Public Transit Association should advise their members of the circumstances of this accident and, in cooperation with the U.S. DOT, notify railroads and public highway entities about the importance of exchanging information regarding railroad/highway grade crossings.

Signal Training

A primary component of the communication issue in this accident was the misunderstanding of the operation of the railroad and highway signal systems by personnel responsible for their design, operation and maintenance. Understanding is an integral element of an effective communication process, and training has proven to be an effective method of developing understanding. However, the Safety Board could not locate any training programs

addressing specifically the interaction of these systems at railroad/highway grade crossings. The Safety Board therefore believes that the U.S. Department of Transportation should develop a training program in the design and operation of railroad/highway grade crossings. The program should include the interaction between rail and highway signal systems. Those representatives of the railroads, public entities, and others who design and maintain grade crossing signal systems should be required to complete the training.

Injury and Survival Factors

The bus passengers who were seated the farthest from the impact area received the least severe injuries, and four of those passengers, seated in rows one through four, were uninjured. Those seated in rows eight and nine sustained serious injuries. Five passengers sustaining serious to minor injuries were either standing or running in the aisle outside the impact area when the bus was struck. They could have received injuries from striking obstacles or other passengers. Had standing passengers struck seated passengers, they likely contributed to the injuries sustained by those seated passengers. Most of the fatally and seriously injured passengers were seated in the last four left side rows, which the crash forces and collision intrusion displaced during impact.

Four of the five fatally injured passengers who had been seated in rows 11 and 12 were found outside the bus near the left side windows. These passengers sustained their fatal injuries during the impact sequence by striking the left side interior of the bus body (windows, frames, and roof structures) and not during the ejection. One ejected passenger from row 12 had a 1.2- by 2-inch, L-shaped abrasion on the left side of his face that closely matched the interior window frame next to his seat. In addition, a fatally injured passenger in row 9 sustained 0.2- by 0.5-inch abrasions across the forehead that matched the perforated sound panel pattern on the upper left side of the bus

[39] Highway Accident Report—*Collapse of U.S. 35 Highway Bridge, Point Pleasant, West Virginia, December 15, 1967* (NTSB-HAR-71/1).

interior. The fifth fatally injured passenger who had been seated in the direct impact area was not ejected, but a seat frame had to be cut to extricate this passenger, who sustained fatal skull fractures and brain and crushing internal injuries similar to those suffered by the ejected fatalities.

The Safety Board considers, with the concurrence of the Cook County pathologist, from the similarity of the head injuries that the fatally injured passengers sustained, as well as from the patterned abrasions and contusions received that closely resembled objects within the bus that could have been struck, all fatal injuries were incurred inside the bus. Therefore, the Safety Board concludes that the passengers found outside the bus sustained their fatal injuries during the initial impact sequence and not as a result of being ejected.

CONCLUSIONS

1. Neither the weather, the position of the sun, the track, nor the mechanical condition of the train or of the school bus either caused or contributed to the collision. The train engineer was qualified to perform his duties and was in compliance with the hours-of-service requirements, and the busdriver was trained and experienced to drive school buses. Neither alcohol nor drug use by the train engineer or the school busdriver was a factor in the accident.

2. Emergency response personnel reacted promptly to the emergency and acted effectively and efficiently at the collision site; the emergency response efforts were well coordinated.

3. The guidance or training provided in the Illinois school busdriver training curriculum about vehicle positioning in relation to the roadway is ineffective.

4. Had the school busdriver discerned the combined visual and audible warnings that a train was approaching, she might have had sufficient time to recognize the hazard and move the bus before impact.

5. The methods employed by the school district to identify and evaluate route hazards were ineffective. Furthermore, had the school district ensured that all school busdrivers exchange information about any identified route hazards, such as the short queuing area, the accident busdriver might have avoided the collision.

6. Had the regular and substitute school busdrivers been monitored during their morning routes, school officials might have been aware that the regular school busdrivers habitually stopped on the south side of the Algonquin Road grade crossing to wait for a green indication.

7. The Illinois Department of Transportation had not employed sufficient measures before the accident to prevent vehicles from encroaching on the railroad tracks while stopped at the north side of the grade crossing.

8. During the Safety Board tests, the railroad grade crossing signal system provided 20 seconds or more warning time before the arrival of a train.

9. The installation and use of railroad and highway signal recording devices at interconnected/preemptive grade crossings can improve opportunities for highway and railroad personnel to determine if the signals are coordinated and operating properly.

10. The highway traffic signal hardware (heads, controllers, masts, posts, and loop detectors) conformed to design standards and operated as intended, but the highway signal system did not provide sufficient time for northbound traffic on Algonquin Road to clear the grade crossing.

11. The highway traffic signal system before the collision provided a green indication for northbound Algonquin Road for 2 to 4 seconds based on the postaccident testing, or for 2 to 6 seconds based on the highway signal system programming.

12. Had a data base containing grade crossing signal system information been available after this accident, the States could have more readily identified and then inspected specific crossings to ensure that the signal systems posed no hazards.

13. The Illinois Department of Transportation had programmed its highway signal system without applying the minimum warning time information from the railroad.

14. Had an effective communication system existed between the Illinois Department of Transportation (IDOT) and the railroads about interconnected signal systems, IDOT, its contractors, and the Illinois Commerce Commission might have understood that the railroad had provided through the thumb wheel setting only the FRA minimum requirement of 20 seconds warning time before the arrival of a train at the grade crossing.

15. Had a coordinated program to ensure effective communication between transportation modes about all aspects of grade crossing safety been in operation, the ineffective communication between IDOT and the railroad might never have occurred.

16. The passengers found outside the bus sustained their fatal injuries during the initial impact sequence and not as a result of being ejected.

PROBABLE CAUSE

The National Transportation Safety Board determines that the probable cause of the collision was that the busdriver had positioned the school bus so that it encroached upon the railroad tracks because of the failure of: 1) the Illinois Department of Transportation to recognize the short queuing area on northbound Algonquin Road and to take corrective action; 2) the Illinois Department of Transportation to recognize the insufficient time of the green signal indication for vehicles on northbound Algonquin Road before the arrival of a train at the crossing; and 3) the Transportation Joint Agreement School District 47/155 to identify route hazards and to provide its drivers with alternative instructions for such situations. Contributing to the accident was the failure of the Illinois Department of Transportation and its contractors, the Illinois Commerce Commission, and the railroads to have a communication system that ensures understanding of the integration and working relationship of the railroad and highway signal systems.

RECOMMENDATIONS

As a result of its investigation of this accident, the National Transportation Safety Board makes the following recommendations:

--to the U.S. Secretary of Transportation:

Develop a comprehensive and periodic railroad/highway grade crossing safety inspection program to be conducted jointly by railroads and public entities and also require railroads and public entities to coordinate any changes to railroad/highway grade crossings before implementation. (I-96-6)

Notify, in cooperation with the American Association of State Highway and Transportation Officials, the National Association of County Engineers, the American Public Works Association, the Institute of Transportation Engineers, the Association of American Railroads, the American Short Line Railroad Association, and the American Public Transit Association, railroads and public entities about the importance of exchanging information about railroad/ highway grade crossings. (I-96-7)

Develop a common glossary of railroad/highway grade crossing terms and disseminate this glossary to railroads and public entities. (I-96-8)

Develop a training program in the design and operation of railroad/ highway grade crossings that includes the interaction between rail and highway signal systems. Require representatives of the railroads, public entities, and others who design and maintain grade crossing signal systems to complete the training program. (I-96-9)

Require the use and maintenance of railroad and highway traffic signal recording devices on all new and improved installations at railroad/ highway grade crossings that have active warning train detection systems and are interconnected/preempted to highway signal systems. These devices should record sufficient parameters to allow railroad and highway personnel to readily determine that the highway signals and railroad-activated warning devices are coordinated and operating properly. Require that the information from these devices be used during comprehensive and periodic joint inspections. (I-96-10)

Require that existing recording devices for railroad and highway signals systems at interconnected/preempted grade crossings be retained or upgraded as necessary. Require that these recording devices be maintained and that the information from these devices be used during the comprehensive and periodic joint inspections. (I-96-11)

--to the Federal Highway Administration:

Develop guidelines and amend the *Manual on Uniform Traffic Control Devices for Streets and Highways* to provide methods to delineate the area (zone) that a train, or its cargo, or both, may occupy on the track or tracks of a railroad grade crossing so motorists have visual reference points that enable them to ascertain whether their vehicle is encroaching on the travel path of the train, or its cargo, or both. (H-96-40)

Disseminate safety information, in cooperation with the National Highway

Traffic Safety Administration and Operation Lifesaver, Inc., once guidelines are developed, to national, State, police, public service, and safety agencies for them to use in developing a training and education module that informs motorists how to recognize the area (zone) that a train and/or its cargo may occupy on the track or tracks of a railroad grade crossing. (H-96-41)

Cooperate with the Federal Railroad Administration in the review and modification of the existing parameters of the National Highway-Rail Crossing Inventory to ensure that it meets the needs of both railroad and highway users. (H-96-42)

--to the Federal Railroad Administration:

In cooperation with the Federal Highway Administration, review and modify the existing parameters of the National Highway-Rail Crossing Inventory to ensure that it meets the needs of both railroad and highway users. Include, as a minimum, information on highway/railroad grade crossings having preemptive or interconnected signals. Once modified, review and update the information annually. (R-96-50)

--to the National Highway Traffic Safety Administration:

Determine what effect school bus sound attenuation materials have on the ability of a busdriver to discern both interior and exterior audible warnings (H-96-43)

Disseminate safety information, in cooperation with the Federal Highway Administration and the Operation Lifesaver, Inc., once guidelines are developed, to national, State, police, public service, and safety agencies for them to use in developing a training and education module that informs motorists how

to recognize the area (zone) that a train and/or its cargo may occupy on the track or tracks of a railroad grade crossing. (H-96-44)

--to the State of Illinois:

Advise school busdrivers of the circumstances of this accident and provide the busdrivers with practical training about vehicle positioning on the road, especially at railroad/highway grade crossings. (H-96-45)

--to the Illinois Department of Transportation:

Review and modify the highway design for all railroad/highway grade crossings in Illinois to ensure that vehicles have adequate space and time to clear the crossing before the arrival of a train. (H-96-46)

Train Illinois Department of Transportation personnel and contractors involved in the design, inspection, and maintenance of highway signals at railroad/highway crossings to ensure that they understand the integration and working relationship of the railroad and highway signal systems. (H-96-47)

--to the Transportation Joint Agreement School District 47/155:

Develop and implement a program for the identification of school bus route hazards and routinely monitor and evaluate all regular and substitute school busdrivers (H-96-48)

--to the National Association of State Directors of Pupil Transportation Services:

Advise your members of the circumstances of this accident and provide guidance about vehicle positioning on the road, especially at railroad/ highway grade crossings. (H-96-49)

Develop guidelines for the appropriate placement of radio speakers and use of radios on school buses and disseminate these guidelines to your members. (H-96-50)

Advise your members to check their school buses and disable any radio speakers located immediately adjacent to school busdrivers' heads. (H-96-51)

Encourage your members to develop and implement a program for the identification of school bus route hazards and to routinely monitor and evaluate all regular and substitute school busdrivers. (H-96-52)

Advise your members to consider railroad/highway grade crossing accident histories or unusual roadway characteristics when establishing school bus routes. (H-96-53)

--to the American Association of State Highway and Transportation Officials:

Advise your members of the circumstances of this accident and, in cooperation with the U.S. Department of Transportation, notify railroads and public entities about the importance of exchanging information regarding railroad/highway grade crossings. (H-96-54)

--to the National Association of County Engineers:

Advise your members of the circumstances of this accident and, in cooperation with the U.S. Department of Transportation, notify railroads and public entities about the importance of exchanging information regarding rail-

road/highway grade crossings. (H-96-55)

--to the American Public Works Association:

Advise your members of the circumstances of this accident and, in cooperation with the U.S. Department of Transportation, notify railroads and public entities about the importance of exchanging information regarding railroad/highway grade crossings. (H-96-56)

--to the Institute of Transportation Engineers:

Advise your members of the circumstances of this accident and, in cooperation with the U.S. Department of Transportation, notify railroads and public entities about the importance of exchanging information regarding railroad/highway grade crossings. (H-96-57)

--to the Association of American Railroads:

Advise your members of the circumstances of this accident and, in cooperation with the U.S. Department of Transportation, notify railroads and public entities about the importance of exchanging information regarding railroad/highway grade crossings. (R-97-51)

--to the American Short Line Railroad Association:

Advise your members of the circumstances of this accident and, in cooperation with the U.S. Department of Transportation, notify railroads and public entities about the importance of exchanging information regarding railroad/highway grade crossings. (R-96-52)

--to the American Public Transit Association:

Advise your members of the circumstances of this accident and, in cooperation with the U.S. Department of Transportation, notify railroads and public entities about the importance of exchanging information regarding railroad/highway grade crossings. (R-96-58)

--to Operation Lifesaver, Inc.:

Disseminate safety information, in cooperation with the Federal Highway Administration and the National Highway Traffic Safety Administration, once guidelines are developed, to national, State, police, public service, and safety agencies for them to use in developing a training and education module that informs motorists how to recognize the area (zone) that a train and/or its cargo may occupy on the track or tracks of a railroad grade crossing. (H-96-59)

BY THE NATIONAL TRANSPORTATION SAFETY BOARD

JAMES E. HALL
Chairman

ROBERT T. FRANCIS II
Vice Chairman

JOHN A. HAMMERSCHMIDT
Member

JOHN J. GOGLIA
Member

GEORGE W. BLACK, JR.
Member

October 29, 1996

APPENDIX A

Investigation Information

Investigation

The National Transportation Safety Board was notified of this accident at approximately 8:30 a.m. on October 25, 1995. Accident investigators dispatched from the Safety Board's Chicago, Illinois, regional office arrived at approximately 9 a.m. on October 25, 1995, and investigators from the Safety Board's headquarters in Washington, D.C., and the regional offices in Atlanta, Georgia, and Arlington, Texas, arrived on the scene that afternoon. A 19-person team conducted the on-scene investigation.

Participating in the investigation were representatives of the Federal Highway Admin- istration, the Federal Railroad Administration, the Illinois Department of Transportation, the Illinois Commerce Commission, the Transportation Joint Agreement School District, the Union Pacific Railroad Company, the Illinois State Police, the McHenry County Sheriff's Department, the Fox River Grove Police Department, Navistar International, Amtran Corporation, and Harmon Industries.

Hearing/Deposition

The Safety Board held a public hearing in conjunction with this investigation on January 17-19, 1996.

APPENDIX B

Injuries	Busdriver	Bus passengers	Traincrew	Train passengers	Total
AIS-0 none	0	4	3	120	127
AIS-1 minor	1	14	0	0	15
AIS-2 moderate	0	4	0	0	4
AIS-3 serious	0	1	0	0	1
AIS-4 severe	0	5	0	0	5
AIS-5 critical	0	7	0	0	7
Total	1	35	3	120	159

Injuries in this table have been coded to the revised 1990 Abbreviated Injury Scale of the American Association for Automotive Medicine, which is the standard system of assessing injury severity.

Abbreviated Injury Scale Table

APPENDIX C
Rail Signal System Information

Harmon HXP-1: General

The Harmon Crossing Processor, Model HXP-1, is a microprocessor-based crossing control system that provides constant warning (CW) times by calculating the speed of the train and its arrival time at the crossing. An RCA 1802 microprocessor chip, the heart of the system, activates the crossing signals by looking at voltage and current levels as well as phase relationship, calculating their rate of change, and determining whether or not the rate of change is sufficient to activate the crossing signals providing the warning time required. The warning time is set by adjusting the warning time (WT) switch with the approach terminations. The WT is limited by the physical distance to the approach terminations.

The microprocessor determines when HXP is to go in high signal or low phase detection. By monitoring voltage increase (RX), the microprocessor causes the crossing control DC voltage Motion Detection (MD) relay to drop, activating the crossing signals when RX voltage increases to 110 or above (RX voltage is set at 100 during initial setup). The microprocessor also monitors the phase relationship between voltage and current, causing the MD relay voltage to drop, activating the crossing signals when the phase angle is below specified limits.

By installing an optional plug-in recorder board into the HXP cabinet, the HXP-1 can record train movement within the confines of the approaches to the highway/rail crossing.

The Recorder Circuit Board (RCB) is an optional HXP-1 module primarily intended for system troubleshooting. It is non-vital[1] in design and has no effect on operation of the HXP. Data are stored in the RCB in three different forms: the train record log, the event buffer log, and the train data log.

The train record log contains a record of the current status of the HXP, along with 222 lines of events, including status lines of the day, time, cabinet number, bi/uni-directional (BI/UNI) switch position, CW/MD switch position, WT, switch settings, and RX pot value. A new status line is generated whenever a variable changes. The train record also logs three calculated train speeds on the approach, the WT, and remarks intended to aid in understanding the data. The three speeds calculated are: initial speed detected on the approach; speed when the island circuit is deenergized; and average speed on the approach calculated when the initial speed is detected until the island circuit deenergizes. These data are retained with power removed.

The event buffer log shows the status of the HXP and records event changes to either the MD,[2] island circuit (ISL), or constant warning enable (CWE) along with corresponding RX and phase values. This log has 256 event lines. The data are not retained with power removed.

The train data log contains the same information as the event buffer log except that it records events twice every second for a maximum of 128 seconds, or 256 events. This log can be used to monitor the RX and phase response during a train move. The data are not retained with power removed.

Data stored in the RCB can be retrieved with any 80-column printer that has an ASCII character set and is RS232C interfaced. Laptop personal computers are ideal means of retrieving, storing, and printing out these data.

---

[1] Any circuit the function of which does not affect the safety of train operations (AAR).

[2] This circuit is designed to detect the motion of a train as it moves through the crossing approach circuit.

A secondary means of viewing the last (most recent) 9 lines of the train record log is provided by means of a thumb wheel switch located on the front edge of the RCB (to select the event line) and the LED display (to view the data). With or without a RCB, the warning time of the most recent train move is available on the LED display, when the display switch is rotated to the WT position.

HXP-1 Operating Principles

During each loop of the HXP operating program, essential track and operating parameters are sequentially tested for proper operation. If any function fails its test, an error code is generated. Any time an error is generated, the MD relay voltage is eliminated (which activates the crossing warning system), a delay timer is initiated (which will prevent the recovery of the relay drive voltage for 25 seconds), and the CPU is reset. The MD relay drive can never recover until the fault is corrected.

Track-related parameters, such as signal amplitude and current and phase (which are combined to produce the RX voltage), are monitored through two separate input channels and stored in diverse form (true and complement) in independent locations. Vital calculations are stored in separate true and complement form, and all data and calculations are cross-checked and verified to be within proper limits. Any discrepancy will produce an error code which will eliminate the MD relay drive voltage.

The CPU operating program loop time is critical to the proper operation of the HXP and is tested to complete its cycle, on time, within a 3.8ms window. Failing this test, the CPU will be reset, and the MD relay drive voltage eliminated. The CPU clock frequency is tested by means of a vital narrow band filter. Any variation of the CPU clock frequency beyond the filter limits will cause the MD relay drive voltage to be permanently eliminated.

The following are some hardware tests that the CPU performs on a regular basis:

- During each program loop cycle, a CPU register test on internal registers verifies that these registers can be written to end read back correctly.

- A test of the RAM is performed every 16 seconds to verify that each byte can be written to and read back correctly.

- A complete test of ROM is performed every 26 seconds, using a 16-bit checksum on each 256-byte block of memory.

- An test of the ROM is performed about every 1.8 hours, using a 16-bit CRC on each 512-byte block of memory to verify that there are no changes to the operating program.

- Power supply voltages are tested each program loop cycle.

- Approach Length Warning Time, LIA, TC switches, and the RX potentiometer are all provided with dual outputs that are compared during each program loop cycle to validate requested values.

- Track data is monitored each loop cycle to identify variations which represent train movement. Some of the parameters calculated are train location, speed, and direction. Track data is averaged for 4 seconds (eight loops), to allow the speed and distance parameters to stabilize, before prediction of train time to island is predicted.

In summary, because of the dual information input paths, the diversity of locations, the manner of data storage, the many hardware checks regularly performed by the CPU, the frequency test of the CPU clock, and the strict limitation of loop cycle timing imposed upon the CPU, it is not possible for the HXP, as a result of internal failures, to produce MD relay voltage yet fail to activate the warning system in a timely manner.

APPENDIX D
Highway Traffic Signal System Information

The Algonquin Road intersection was controlled by a fully traffic actuated signal system. The components of the signal installation included the following equipment: signal heads, pedestrian signal heads, pedestrian push buttons, signal posts, mast arms, internally illuminated blank out regulatory signs, vehicle loop detectors, controller and cabinet, conduit, cable, and hand-holes. The traffic signal controller at Algonquin Road was part of a closed loop traffic signal system that included a master controller to the west at US 14 and Lincoln Avenue and a traffic signal controller to the east at US 14 and Illinois State Route 22. The traffic signal installation at Algonquin Road provided six separate vehicle phases and two pedestrian phases with turn movement overlaps for:

- Northbound traffic

- Southbound traffic

- Southeast-bound traffic

- Northwest-bound traffic

- Southeast- and Northwest-bound left turns

- Two separate pedestrian phases, movements crossing US 14 on the east side of the intersection and crossing Algonquin Road on the south side of the intersection. In addition, a north to southeast-bound right turn overlap appears in conjunction with the northwest to southbound left turn phase during normal operation.

1. Normal Sequence — This sequence operates the intersection at all times that the signal is not being preempted by railroad or emergency vehicles.

   A. Coordinated Operation - When the system operates in the semi-actuated mode from 5:45 a.m. until 10 p.m.,

the mainline detectors are inoperative. This type of operation includes the display of two separate nonconflicting phases on an on-demand basis for the intersecting roadways.

   B. Fully Actuated Sequence — When the system operates in the free mode from 10 p.m. to 5:45 a.m., mainline detectors for US 14 are turned on and all other detectors remain active. In addition, the pedestrian detection associated with the non-conflicting mainline coordinated phase is turned on until the controller receives a preemption call.

2. Railroad Preemption - The railroad preemption sequence takes priority control over the intersection once a call to the traffic controller is received that a train is approaching the intersection. This call is received via a hardwire connection from the railroad control bungalow to the traffic signal control cabinet. Once the call is received and all of the conflicting vehicle and/or pedestrian phases have terminated with their proper clearance intervals, the controller allows the northbound Algonquin Road phase to appear green while everything else is omitted.

3. Emergency Vehicle Preemption - The emergency vehicle preemption sequence is activated once an emergency vehicle call is received in the traffic signal controller. This call is received via a high-intensity light emitter mounted on the emergency vehicle and a detector mounted on, or near, the traffic control signal. Once the emergency or priority vehicle is detected, the detector relays a

signal to a phase selector which is connected to the signal controller. This phase selector then checks the status of the controller. The selector either extends the green interval for the emergency vehicle or terminates the green on the street or streets opposing the emergency vehicle after all proper clearance intervals for vehicle or pedestrian traffic have terminated.

The emergency vehicle preemption sequence takes lower priority control of the intersection than the railroad preemption sequence. For example, if an emergency vehicle preemption is received by the traffic controller and a subsequent railroad preemption call is received, the railroad preemption overrides the emergency vehicle call. After all proper clearance intervals for vehicle or pedestrian traffic have terminated, the controller allows the northbound Algonquin Road phase to appear green.

Between January 1990 and October 1994 the three intersections were operated by Multisonics controllers. During that period, IDOT and their contractor were unable to operate the traffic signals as a coordinated system. Therefore, the pedestrian clearance indications would appear only if a pedestrian push button were pushed. Without the pedestrian push button

activation, during the approach of a train, the green track clearance signal for Algonquin Road would have appeared after the 4.5 seconds of amber and 1.5 seconds of all red (6 seconds). If the pedestrian push button was activated, prior to the approach of a train, a 12-second pedestrian clearance time (flashing DON'T WALK) would appear in addition to the 6 seconds (solid DON'T WALK) for the amber and red traffic signals before the green track clearance green for Algonquin Road would be displayed. In October of 1994, the three Multisonics controllers were replaced with Econolite ASC-8000 controllers (the master controller was placed at Lincoln Avenue).

At that time, the three controllers began operating as a coordinated system. When the Econolite controllers were in coordinated operation, between 5:45 a.m. and 10 p.m., the 12-second pedestrian clearance interval would be displayed every cycle even without pedestrian push button activation. The total time for this cycle would be 18 seconds before a green traffic signal would be displayed for Algonquin Road vehicles waiting in the queue area. Between 10 p.m. and 5:45 a.m. the signal system was fully actuated and the 12-second pedestrian clearance phase would be eliminated unless a pedestrian push button were pushed.

APPENDIX E

Excerpts from National Standards School Transportation Standards: Recommended Procedures for School Bus Drivers at Railroad Grade Crossings

General

1. The driver of any school bus, whether carrying passengers or not, must before crossing any track or tracks, bring the bus to a full and complete stop within not less than fifteen feet or more than fifty feet from the rails nearest the front of the bus.

2. When drivers are making stops for railroad crossings, they shall carefully observe traffic and reduce speed far enough in advance to avoid trapping other motorists in panic stops or rear-end collisions with the bus. On multiple lane roadways, no such stops shall be made in the center or left-hand lanes.

3. No special signs, signals or flashers designated for use on school buses shall be activated while the bus is stopping for this purpose. Note: The option to activate hazard lights or four-way flashers is at the discretion of the transportation agency or regulated by state statute.

4. The driver, when stopped, shall fully open the service door and driver's window, and must, after the stop and while so stopped, listen and look in both directions along the track or tracks for approaching engines, trains or cars. Upon resumption of motion, the service door may be closed.

5. If the view of the track or tracks, for a distance of one thousand feet in either direction is not clear or is obstructed in any way, no portion of the bus may be propelled onto the tracks until, by personal inspection, the driver has made certain that no train is approaching. In no instance may a signal indicating safety be considered as conclusive or serve to abrogate this precaution.

6. Drivers shall, in every instance, cross in a gear that will not changing gears while traversing such crossing and shall not, under any circumstances, shift gears while actually crossing tracks or crossings.

7. In the event that a train has passed over the crossing, no bus driver shall drive the bus onto the track or tracks until such train has sufficiently cleared the crossing so that the driver is certain that no train, hidden by the first train, is approaching on an adjacent track.

8. For improved hearing, all noisy equipment (fans, etc.) should be off until the bus has cleared the crossing.

At Crossings Controlled by Signals Only

1. In addition to the above, the driver of a school bus which has stopped at any railroad tracks where there are red lights and/or bells in operation, shall not proceed across such track or tracks unless by authorization from a law enforcement officer or train personnel, though this does not relieve the driver of personal responsibility for safe crossing.

2. In the event that switching operations or stopped trains delay the use of the crossing for frequent or extended periods of time, complaint should be made through proper channels to management and traffic authorities.

At Crossings Controlled by Crossing Gates or Barriers

1. No bus driver shall drive the bus through, around or under any crossing gate or barrier

at a railroad crossing while such gate or barrier is closed or being opened or closed.

2. The bus driver must never accept a lack of movement as indicating that the device is either in or out of order or not properly operating, but must always take a crossing as a conclusive warning of danger and must not cross the tracks until the bus driver has conclusively ascertained that no train is approaching.

Weather Conditions

During wet, stormy or foggy weather, before placing part of the bus on the tracks, the driver must know conclusively that the crossing can be made safely. Any use of flares, etc., in addition to warning signals or devices maintained at such railroad crossings, must be taken as an additional warning of danger.

Management of Passengers

When any school bus must stop to cross any track, all passengers must be silent until the crossing is completed. A signal for silence shall be given by the driver in whatever manner is deemed suitable.

Adapted from Fact Sheet, "Recommended Procedures for School Bus Drivers at Railroad Grade Crossings," revised, School Transportation Section, 1984, National Safety Council, 1121 Spring Lake Dr., Itasca, IL 60143-3201.

APPENDIX F

Task Force Recommendations

A. *Short-Term Recommendations*

1) State transportation agencies (or other State agencies, if appropriate) should formally agree to be the focal point in the State to ensure proper coordination between highway authorities and railroads regarding the interconnection of grade crossing warning devices and highway traffic signals, and consideration of the storage distance between the tracks and the parallel highway. The responsibilities of the agency, as a focal point, would be to:

   a) Develop, distribute, and continually update a list of State and local highway authorities and railroad contacts who should be involved in the planning, design, construction, operation, and inspection of grade crossing warning devices interconnected with nearby highway traffic signals;

   b) Serve as a clearinghouse for collecting and disseminating to State and local highway authorities and railroads all pertinent information necessary for the planning, design, construction, and safe operation of grade crossings in close proximity to highway-highway intersections;

   c) Develop guidelines which recommend that, on at least an annual basis, State and local highway authorities and railroads and/or transit agencies conduct joint inspections of the timing and operation of highway traffic signals that are interconnected to nearby grade crossing warning devices; and,

   d) Coordinate with State and local school transportation officials, operators of public transit or intercity buses, and trucking organizations to help ensure

that drivers are familiar with the operation of interconnected signals and are aware of any storage space limitations at grade crossings on their routes. This information exchange would be carried out in cooperation with Operation Lifesaver.

2) State and local highway authorities should initiate engineering studies to determine if safety improvements are warranted at grade crossings near highway-highway intersections where there is no interconnection and *where there is limited storage distance.* Emphasis should be given to locations with STOP sign control at the highway-highway intersection, where storage space is less than that required to accommodate the longest legal vehicle permitted to use the highway, and where accident potential is greater due to high volumes of highway and/or rail traffic.

3) State and local highway authorities, through coordination with the railroads, should ensure that storage space is a significant consideration early in the planning and design processes where physical changes are being proposed to the highway or railroad at interconnected signal locations.

4) FHWA and FRA field staff should initiate regional conferences throughout the country for highway agencies and railroads to specifically discuss grade crossing safety issues, including interconnected signals and storage practices.

B. *Long-Term Recommendations*

1) The FHWA should convene a technical working group that includes representatives of rail crossing safety organizations to

review existing standards and guidelines and develop new ones, if appropriate, on grade crossing safety including the following issues: when interconnected signals should be used, minimum clearance green time, the existing 20-second minimum warning time, critical storage distance, use of near side traffic signals, joint highway agency/railroad/transit inspections, and stopping on tracks. One of the outputs of this group could be recommended additions and/or changes to the MUTCD, the *Railroad-Highway Grade Crossing Handbook*, or other appropriate guidance documents. The group should be established and hold its initial organizational meeting by June 1, 1996, and submit proposed standards/ guidelines within a year.